Psychic Pets

Solving Paranormal Mysteries

Dinah Roseberry

Schiffer Publishing Ltd®

4880 Lower Valley Road   Atglen, Pennsylvania   19310

Designed by Stephanie Daugherty
Type set in Airstream/New Baskerville BT
ISBN: 978-0-7643-3398-9
Printed in China

Schiffer Books are available at special discounts for bulk purchases for sales promotions or premiums. Special editions, including personalized covers, corporate imprints, and excerpts can be created in large quantities for special needs. For more information contact the publisher:

Published by Schiffer Publishing Ltd.
4880 Lower Valley Road
Atglen, PA 19310
Phone: (610) 593-1777; Fax: (610) 593-2002
E-mail: Info@schifferbooks.com

For the largest selection of fine reference books on this and related subjects, please visit our web site at

www.schifferbooks.com

We are always looking for people to write books on new and related subjects. If you have an idea for a book please contact us at the above address.

This book may be purchased from the publisher. Include $5.00 for shipping. Please try your bookstore first. You may write for a free catalog.

In Europe, Schiffer books are distributed by
Bushwood Books
6 Marksbury Ave.
Kew Gardens
Surrey TW9 4JF England
Phone: 44 (0) 20 8392-8585; Fax: 44 (0) 20 8392-9876
E-mail: info@bushwoodbooks.co.uk
Website: www.bushwoodbooks.co.uk

Contents

Dedication

For Peter Schiffer,

—who probably only now knows just how bizarre this world we live in really is. You're missed, Peter. And that's a learning experience...and an opportunity.

And I can't forget my own troop:

Tessa, Spiderman, Rufus, and Murphy O'Reilley

Human Acknowledgments

In one way or another, all the people listed here helped me during my quest to solve the animal mystery known as animal communications. Is it solved? Don't have a clue, but still, without the help and guidance from these fine people and places, things would never have gotten as far as they did!

Thank you to: Angela Katsiaginnis, Ann, Atglen Veterinarian Hospital, Beckah Boyd, Bob Meyer, Bruce Waters, Carroll Roseberry, Carol Starr, Chester County SPCA (PA), Cindy, David Wells, Debra Prosser, Donna Baker, Donna Doyle, Elaine's Haunted Dinner Theater, Gerri Gassert, Ginger Doyle, Hope Pollock, Jackie Wasdick, Jan Reeps, Jesse Rothacker, Karen Choppa, Kat Driver, Katie Boyd, Kim Ritchie, Humane League of Lancaster County (PA), Kaye Ames School for Dogs, Laurie Hull, Lenora, Lee Prosser, Lisa Smith, Lisa Williams, Marjorie, Mark Nelson, Mark Sarro, Marla Brooks, Mary Gasparo, Robbin Van Pelt, the Schiffers (Peter, Pete, and Nancy), Stacey McNutt, Stephanie Daugherty, Tina Skinner, Tom and Arlene D'Agostino, Victoria Gross, West Chester Veterinary Medical Center (PA), Yvonne Abwender.

A very special thank you to animal communicator, Anita Curtis. This book would not have been possible without you.

Animal Acknowledgments

My Animal Spirit Guides: **Leo and Lee.**

Amish horses, Angus, Belle, Bentley, BJ, Cape May Kitty, Cooneys, Elwood, George, Gracie, Kalli, Latté, Lilly, Murphy O'Reiley, Pipsqueak, Rob Roy, Rock Creature, Rufus, Squirrel, Snake, Solo, Spiderman, Tessa, Zira.

Foreword: Anita Curtis, Animal Communicator

I have just finished reading the draft of Dinah Roseberry's new book, *Psychic Pets;* Dinah's travels through the world of animal communications were presented in a matter-of-fact and fun-loving way, with just the right amount of awe and respect.

The powerful Leo and bouncy Lee have led her down paths that have enhanced her previous journeys into the spirit world as well as the animal world. The crotchety Bentley managed to keep her grounded in the land of here and now.

Here, a ghostly energy flows into the barn to keep the horse company. Anita often has visitations from her loved ones who have passed over, so her animals are well acquainted with them, too. *Photo courtesy of Anita Curtis.*

A very friendly BB is always on the lookout for a carrot—but that's not the only communication that's passed between her and Anita. *Photo courtesy of Anita Curtis.*

I read with interest the saga of Tessa and Spiderman, rooting for one, and then the other. I knew what was going to happen, since I was there (I'm not going to give the end away here—you'll have to read it yourself.), but Dinah's storytelling skills had me caught up in the tale as if I were hearing it for the first time.

Dinah's love of animals shows itself throughout *Psychic Pets*. When I first met her at an animal communications workshop, I knew she was a ghost hunter and author. I thought she was probably doing research, and I was glad to have her in the class. A book raising the awareness that animals can think and feel is always a wonderful tool for them. However, Dinah shared the story of the Amish horse early in the workshop, and the passion in her voice told me that she was truly there to learn to hear the animals for the sake of helping, healing, bonding, and loving them.

It is a great honor to have traveled beside Dinah on this part of her journey. The animals continue

to teach me life's lessons every day, and my hand is out to those who would like to learn with me. Dinah took my hand and lived up to learning from the wisdom of the animals.

~Anita Curtis
Author of: *Animal Wisdom:*
How to Hear the Animals and
A Second Chance to Say Goodbye

For more information about Anita Curtis and her varied workshops and services, visit her on the Internet at www.anitacurtis.com.

Anita's horses are definitely not camera shy. *Photo courtesy of Anita Curtis.*

Introduction

"I believe that everyone has the ability to use telepathy, especially those of us who are totally devoted to animals and who love them deeply."

~Donna Doyle, Animal Communicator

"Go to hell! You don't know nothin'!" was my first communication with my first client.

I didn't know how to respond—or even if I *should*. This "instruction," of course, had to be my crazed mind thinking I had the power to talk to animals when indeed I was just a dazed nutcase. But doubt remained. Could it possibly be my mind? I knew, though, that you couldn't make this stuff up. I could actually see the bird, a lovely cockatiel of gray, white, and yellow, pacing back and forth in my mind's eye—giving me the *evil eye* at each turn. Grumbling and sarcastic. Ready to

take me on in a second should I choose to disagree with his knowing of my *not* knowing "nothin'."

Marla Brooks, the celebrated ghost hunter, author of the *Ghosts of Hollywood* series, *Workplace Spells*, and the "hostess with the mostess" on Para-X Radio's *Stirring the Cauldron*, hadn't warned me about her family sidekick prior to the reading. She was trying to help me out by giving me practice for my newly-learned skill of animal communications. Did *she* have an animal for *me*! Bentley. I should talk to him, she advised very seriously. He would be good practice for me.

But surprise (and a feeling of "Yikes!") swept me away at first contact in a breeze of self doubt. I was just getting the hang of how the animal messages came to me. It was an odd process and oftentimes felt a bit like daydreaming. This was a scary thing when you were working with people who didn't have a concept of communicating with animals and expected *me* to. My personal questions were always: Is this a daydream that my mind is making up to suit my thoughts at this particular moment? Am I really seeing this animal and hearing it talk to me—in my own voice no less? Or have I lost my mind? Most definitely.

Bentley scared me. He was my first actual "consumer" outside my circle of animal communications friends who were all learning the skill. We'd been practicing on each other's animals (dead and alive).

Bentley, a Hollywood cockatiel, is quite the character. He makes no bones about telling anyone who bothers him to "Go to Hell!" *Photo courtesy of Marla Brooks.*

12

But this Hollywood bird—he was different. He had a force within him that was to be respected, and if I understood him correctly, feared. This was a bird who meant business. As I type this, I can see his little head bobbing up and down with an emphatic *yes*. *Don't mess with the bird* was his motto. Make no mistake, Bentley would be in my future for some time to come.

In the Beginning

But let me take a moment to allow you to understand how I came to be sitting in front of my computer looking at a photo of the lovely Bentley as I listened to his little voice beat me up and tear my ego into tiny pieces. I wasn't always an animal communicator. In fact, it wasn't on my agenda to *ever* become one. I was a ghost hunter.

My quest for the spirits of the animals actually came due to an unfortunate experience. I'm afraid that it was a turmoil-filled cascade of negative emotion and out-and-out fury that made me not only wonder at the miracle of the world beyond for animals, but feel the aching need of justice touch my heart—no, *punch my heart* was a more apt description.

I saw my first actual animal ghost in the form of a cat at Elaine's Haunted Mansion in Cape May, New Jersey, as I was writing *Cape May Haunts*. At that time, I was in such awe that I was able to actually *see* a ghost, that little more came to mind—i.e., its reason for being there and that it was an animal that might have something to say. It wasn't that I felt a need to communicate with *that* particular cat. I didn't really want to attach myself to its history. I didn't need to feel its pain or make right its circumstances before, or after, death. I was just there to witness it and develop my own abilities to perceive ghosts—or at least see into the world beyond our living one if the skill was so afforded me.

And then came a time that I was researching areas of Pennsylvania for a ghost book I was planning to write. It wasn't my first (or even my second or third) choice to include animal ghosts as a topic

in the spooky happenings in this fair state. There were certainly sufficient historic hauntings and contemporary spooks to fill ten books—enough to peak the interest of ghost enthusiasts for eons. But then something surprising happened to me. Well, if truth be told, not surprising but horrific—and not to me, but to an unfortunate animal crossing my mundane path.

In this bedroom at Elaine's Haunted Theater and B&B in Cape May, New Jersey, I saw my first animal ghost during an interview with owner Ron Long and psychic Laurie Hull for the ghost book, *Cape May Haunts*. The spirit of a gray cat scooted around the corner and out the door as we were talking. The electromagnetic field meters we were using (EMF) displayed readings indicative of ghostly activity. It was an exciting time for me and well before I'd realized that people could communicate with animals.

A Heat From Hell

It was the summer of 2007 in Intercourse and Paradise—a truly beautiful and historic area of Lancaster County, Pennsylvania. And it was hot. No, hot doesn't touch it. Blistering. *Hmmm.* Even that seems too little. Let me be scientific here by saying that the heat index via the local news channel was telling me that though the thermometer was showing 102 degrees Fahrenheit, it felt like 110. And oh, can humidity be a nasty thing.

My husband and I were on our way home from the York, Pennsylvania, area and we'd planned to avoid traffic by taking a route through Paradise, Pennsylvania, along Route 340 to 772.

My first bout of fury came when I saw that, though the temperatures were hellish, Amish

A scene from the beautiful countryside in Intercourse, Pennsylvania, where the Amish use horse and buggy rides as a means of income. Tourism is booming—particularly in the summer when temperatures have been known to go over 100 degrees F.

tourism was booming and horses were being forced to drag wagons filled to the brim with visitors through the lazy historic town. (For those not familiar with the Amish folk, they are a group of people involved in a somewhat radical Christian religion, known for their resistance to

15

modern ease. They live simple lives, without cars and televisions or any convenience that might go against what they consider to be against God. Their transportation consists of buggies and wagons drawn by horses.)

I didn't know who to be more angry with—the visitors who were *in* the wagons or the Amish who were driving the horses. Both had equal responsibility in what I personally considered to be animal abuse. Apparently, there are those who feel that animals are not on God's good-guy list.

But that was a minimal fury. As we turned south onto 772, almost immediately, we saw an Amish buggy stopped on the side of the road. An Amish man was standing on the turf of a nearby lawn looking quite perplexed as his horse lay dead on the bright green grass of someone's front yard. In my eyes, he had obviously driven his horse to death—a beautiful young-looking horse. Now he stood on the lawn with the look about him that said, "Now how do I get home?" (This was not my first awareness of animal abuse among this group, but it was the first I'd personally witnessed.)

I exploded in anger and then I started to cry—and that continued all the way home. Once there, I fired off letters to every humane organization I could think of, every local newspaper, and anyone else I thought might muster power. Alas, if my complaints fell on deaf ears or if a glimmer of hope was gleaned, I'll never know. The only kind response I received was from the Humane League of Lancaster County—who were familiar with this type of complaint, but could make no headway though they'd tried and tried.

This is where the first itch of ghostly animal communication desire came into play. I wanted to talk to that dead horse. I wanted to see its ghost. I wanted to apologize for the indignities and cruelty that the human race heaped on this kind, beautiful, and serving creature.

This did not happen at that time, for I didn't know how to do that.

Life went on.

More Animal Tragedy

Days went by, then weeks, then seasons. The spring of 2008 came, and beautiful as it was in many ways, there was the fragrance of death on the breeze. It came to pass that it was time for my seventeen-year-old peek-a-poo, Tessa, to move to the other side. She'd lived a wonderful life with me—love, care, and all the carrots she could eat at her beck and call—but now, her advanced age and severe arthritic pain had taken its toll.

As is usually the case, we'd racked up quite a vet bill trying to care for her, and one weekend, she was in such severe pain, we decided that it was time. She should not be forced to suffer any longer. The arrangements were made quickly and handled expertly by the wonderful folks that tend to the well-being of animals on weekends in the area, the West Chester Emergency Animal Hospital. My husband and I were there with her at the final moment.

But once it was done, I found that I'd not been as ready as I thought for what I'd seen

Tessa, my sweet peek-a-poo, lived a long and happy life, leaving for the otherside in March of 2008 at the age of seventeen.

and felt in those last moments of her life. Guilt attacked me with a vengeance and a force that was nearly debilitating. At the end, I'd expected her to go calmly off to sleep—and she did—but I wasn't prepared for the fact that her eyes would

remain open. Dead glass, the spark of life there one moment, and then gone, in seconds. All this because *I* had taken her life from her. I had chosen to execute her. I took all the guilt of killing the dog I loved into my heart. It felt like murder. That guilt grew. And I wasn't healing. It was a pain I wouldn't have wished on anyone. And I kept it inside, sharing that sentence with no one. For the decision had been mine. I'd killed my Tessa.

Misery was my companion.

Longs Park, Lancaster County, Pennsylvania

Of course, despite the pain of loss, life moves forward yet again. Jobs continue. People eat supper. Paychecks come and go. We do laundry. (Or not.)

I continued to suffer in silence. Relief, though, was around the corner, and I didn't see it coming. It began at my office where I was (and am) senior editor for a paranormal line of books. Everyone knew that I was currently working on a ghost book (wasn't I always?) and the publisher's personal assistant told me about an affair to be held at Longs Park, not too very far from my home. "Ruffin It…A Day in the Park" was an event that was aimed at animal lovers with all proceeds going to benefit the group United Against Puppy Mills. (This is another horrendous area

Anyone who has been to Longs Park in Lancaster County, Pennsylvania, knows that spring time is filled with color and wonder—the perfect place for a dog walk in the park!

18

of abuse that has received much media attention, and that sometimes points to the practices of the Amish in Lancaster, Pennsylvania.) There was to be an animal communicator at this function who was able to talk to animals that had passed over.

Hmmm. An animal communicator—a person who could talk to dead animals. I knew little of this field beyond the television show (*Pet Psychic*) that showed a woman talking to the spirits of live animals in a rather engaging way with a fierce accent that was often delightful. I was intrigued—and fighting a feeling of hope at the possibility of talking to my own little Tessa. Was this real?

My husband and I made plans to go to this event and to enjoy the beautiful Longs Park with its picturesque grounds. Saturday, April 6, 2008, would be a good day. And besides, it was research.

That Saturday, I printed out photos of Tessa on the computer printer and we headed out to the animal event to see what this animal communications thing was all about. How could someone on *this* side, talk to an animal on the *other* side without being a psychic of some sort? This, as far as I knew, wasn't what ghosts and spirits were all about.

Truly A Tale—or Tail—to Tell

Anyone who has been to Longs Park knows that the setting is gorgeous on a sunny spring-like day. The trees are filled with pink floral wonder and the lake glistens in the sun like rippling glass. The temperature was perfect and we arrived right at the opening of the event. There were animal participants as well as people and it was fun to see the reactions of the varied breeds as they strolled their people about. We, of course, were sans dog.

We first walked about to get a lay of the land and then hovered around the table of Animal Communicator Donna Doyle—known as Donna Doolittle to those who used her services. She was energetic and happy as she was setting up her display table offering goodies that were sure to draw in spirit. I recognized the gemstones of spiritual protection from my routine ghost research, but *these* had real value—they were set as jewelry! (Most

female ghost hunters have a yen for this kind of thing...) She advised me that both she and one of her students, Cindy, from the Lancaster nonprofit animal organization, A Tail to Tell, would be giving animal readings. I signed up, telling myself that this was all for the sake of researching my book.

A Tail to Tell does some wonderful things—they rescue dogs that have been brought into the world via puppy mills. I cried when I read the things on their website. This is a place to volunteer, folks. Anyway, when I approached Cindy and handed her the photo of my departed Tessa, she immediately began to cry—her eyes spilled over like faucets. "I don't think I can do this," she said to me. "It's too hard; there is so much worry. Not your worry," she said to me, "but hers. She doesn't want

A Tail to Tell is a pet organization whose mission it is to stop the puppy mills from flourishing in Lancaster County. Breeding for business is not looked upon favorably when the animals are abused in the process.

you to feel guilty. You helped her cross over and she thanks you for that. She'd waited too long to cross over, knowing you needed more time with her, and she was too weak to do it herself. But she wants you to stop grieving. She's still with you. She loves you."

I was amazed. This woman knew nothing about me or my situation. I'd only broken down after a couple weeks of silent grief to tell my husband that, though I knew Tessa was in pain, I felt such guilt. I felt as though I'd killed her. And now Cindy stood before me saying that not only did she know of my feelings, she was there to tell me that this was not so. She had to stop talking to me, though, because she could not handle Tessa's worry for me. It was so strong and so sad. She took me then to Donna Doyle, who was the expert when it came to animals on the other side.

I could tell right away that Donna had been doing this a while and had control of her feelings about life on the other side and death on this one. She

immediately restated what Cindy had said (without having been in earshot of her) and began to answer some of the other questions I had about life on the other side—and our interaction here with that life.

I learned that our other *live* dog (Rufus) was still seeing Tessa (all the time) and this was why he'd seemed so spooked and stressed since her death. In reality, he'd been a basket case since the day she died and having all sorts of serious medical issues. Tessa, on the

Animal Communicator, Donna Doyle with her grandson, Jacob, enjoying the Special Equestrians in Warminster, Pennsylvania. *Photo courtesy of Donna Doyle.*

other hand, didn't immediately understand why all the sadness was in our home and why she was not being treated the same as before. She was still there with us, in her eyes—still doing the nightly walk-about the house to check for … well, whatever she used to check for before we all went to bed. *Why was everyone so sad?* she wanted to know. *Why the tears? What was the problem with Rufus?* Donna communicated to her the situation so that she understood. Though at the time, I

hadn't a clue how she was doing this amazing thing.

The big message Donna relayed was that I needed to get over the guilt and let Tessa go—she was hooked to this place because *I* was not *all right*. As long as I felt as though I'd killed her and as long as I pined for her, wallowing in self-pity, she could not (and would not) move on. She would not abandon me—ever.

She told me much more that comes into play a bit later on, but for now, suffice it to say that I was so impressed (and surprised) with the small details of my relationship with my dogs that were revealed—things that only someone living with us would know—that I could not contain myself. These ladies, there at Longs Park to combat puppy mills, on that very day, could not phantom the difference they'd made in our lives. In my life.

That's Not All Folks
Anita Curtis Steps Up

Of course, that wasn't the end of it. Not only had I seen a ghost animal in the past, but now I knew that people could talk to them on the other side. A chord was struck. Further, I'd found that this was a skill that could be learned. Yes, yes one could talk to all the animals living, but more importantly—this could be a new connection to the world of the paranormal I was so intimately involved with. I wanted to learn to do this, if it were possible.

This is when I became aware of Anita Curtis, an animal communicator for many, many years in the Pennsylvania area. Through her own experiences and advanced training with Jeri Ryan, Ph.D. and Penelope Smith (a pioneer in the animal communications world), Anita honed her abilities to talk to animals (living and dead) and to help educate those around her. Anita was holding a two-

day workshop in Pennsylvania within weeks of my visit to Longs Park. I was determined to gain this skill—after all, I had a dead horse to talk with and many other animals who'd become part of my varied ghost investigations and sightings. And Tessa.

So it came to be that I ended up at Kaye Ames School for Dogs—another wonderful animal resource that incorporates not only workshops like this one,

Kay Ames School for Dogs provides not only training for the local community relating to dogs, but also hosts programs like Anita Curtis' Animal Communication Workshop.

Anita Curtis with her horse and animal companion BB.

but all kinds of training and behavioral disciplines to improve communications between "man and his or her best friend." I'm still finding out how animal organizations and people all somehow just connect—without effort, as though they were all meant to be one big happy family.

I was a bit nervous at first. What if I couldn't do it? Wait a minute…I *knew* I couldn't do it! What if I made a fool of myself? I quickly dismissed that question, because I do that fairly routinely—nothing new. It took me about five minutes to find out that I wasn't the only one in the room with these misgivings. Everyone had the same fears. We all wanted to learn this ability, but feared the worst. It couldn't be done. It was clear in my mind: I can't talk to those on the other side. But a little voice inside said, "Well, maybe; stranger things have happened over the prior years where ghosts were concerned." (Haven't a clue whose voice *that* was!)

Anita Curtis and her star student helper, Jan Reeps, were magnificent teachers and presenters. They were teaching us, they said, what we already knew—just how to use this communication skill whenever we wanted. Within two days I was talking to ghost animals—and quite pleased with myself, because I felt like I had "the knack." I could do this.

And I've been doing it ever since.

1. Getting Into the Spirit of Things

"Intuition is your greatest gift and your greatest guide."

~David Wells, Psychic Medium

I need to give credit where credit is due in all this communicating with the dead. One thing that I learned in the Anita Curtis workshop was the importance of spirit guides. Now this was not a concept unfamiliar to me. In the world of ghost hunting, it's practically impossible not to embrace the notion that there is a God—or greater power, depending on your beliefs—beyond what we can see in this flimsy reality, providing us with angels and/or guides if we so choose to accept help in that manner.

In my early years, though I'd believed in the hereafter, I didn't put too much time into looking for or understanding the "beings of light" out there for my benefit. I was a busy lady. I had a job. I had boyfriends. I had the proverbial ticking clock inside my head. (Ah, now I understand my mother's sentiment of "youth being wasted on the young.") There just wasn't enough time to pursue the things that had value—if, in fact, I'd even had the ability to recognize said things. I hadn't. And to be honest, outside church activities, angels, and spirit guides were not "in" for many in those early years. The stories were not routine unless you traveled in "those circles" of enlightened people. Again, I hadn't.

But once I became involved with ghostly research, I found that meditation had spurred a veritable ability for visualization in me—a way to touch these beings. Also a writer, I had the ability to weave stories in my mind, seeing the landscapes and personalities of everything from foliage to human to animal to fantasy. I didn't have to try real hard. So as I began to study the spirit guides and angels as related by other psychic people and books on the subject, I found that, with a little bit of effort, I could meditate quickly into a visualization exercise that made finding spirit guides and angels pretty simple.

Did I believe I was in touch with real beings during these exercises? At first there was doubt. I'd always been known for an active imagination—I called it being creative. But this was outside the radar. Since I believed in God, I just looked at these intermediary beings as the go-between between me and God—who I didn't have a clear concept of. And maybe they weren't there at all. Maybe it was my mind in a demented or some religious state. I did know that I believed that God, the angels, spirit guides, and other beings of light did not exist as folks living in the clouds above. I knew they were everywhere and right here. But what was this "he" stuff, which indicated that God was of human vision. Not sure—still not clear how you describe *everything* as *something*. At any rate, it was easy to see the beings of light—I couldn't see features, rather they were just tubes of white and golden light hovering around me. And getting into the state where I could see them was straightforward. It was little more than self hypnosis and creative visualization for me.

I mentioned mediation earlier as though this was a quick way for me to reach out to my guides and angels. That's not exactly true. The accepted variation of meditation is something that I don't usually reach. It doesn't matter if I'm sitting, standing, laying down, or standing on my head, I fall asleep when I meditate. It's a cross to bear to be sure. So I've replaced the true meditation with strong visualization, but I still think it can be classified as a kind of meditation—just not the preferred term or method.

I practiced this method as a writer fairly routinely when creating scenes; I've learned to hone it by learning a specific technique I learned in a stress management class—after I changed it to meet my needs.

Finding Your Guides in Animal Communications

Why, you may be asking, is this important? If you want clear communications and also protection from the evil things on the other side (and in this world), you need a team in your corner. For animal communications you need an animal guide. An animal guide is like a supervisor. It will stand by you, helping you when you become frustrated (and you will), and give you tips to move forward with your communications. In some cases, the communication will come through this guide, or be confirmed by this guide, so that you can garnish the right meanings of the things you are seeing, feeling, or "knowing." At other times... not so much.

Note that I am saying "you." Maybe you didn't pick up this book to learn how to communicate with animals, rather just to hear a good story about them. But I'm thinking that you most assuredly have an interest in them, so I'm here to tell you that not only can everyone do this, everyone should. You've stumbled onto a "two-fer" here! Just like people chant to you the importance of being in touch with nature, interacting with the animals on this planet is also imperative. You don't have to do it on a grand scale—that's practically impossible anyway. But you can change the world right in your own backyard. You can alleviate suffering (both human and animal) and feel a sense of purpose that truly connects you to God (or your belief) and to those waiting on the other side. Okay, I'm off the soap box now.

During my class with Anita, she explained this visualization exercise; and I was very excited because I'd been doing this for some time, interacting with my customary spirit guides and angels. I'd already identified my spirit animal that stays with me for my regular lifetime, but was told that there might be another one who would handle the animal communications for me. In fact, I learned, guides came and went in one's life as needed, though there was a core group that stuck around as one muddled through the trials and tribulations of life on earth.

At any rate, the advice Anita provided was important. She said that though you may have a preconceived notion of who your spirit animal guide is or who you'd like it to be, this was not usually the case. She told a humorous story:

"I wanted to become a gazelle but an elephant came to me and I enjoyed mud baths and blowing water over my back through my trunk. It couldn't have been more different from a gazelle. The next time I tried it, a female gorilla came to me. I just gave up after that and enjoyed whoever came to help me. A buzzard came when I wrote how to be a bird of prey in my book, *Animal Wisdom*. I wanted to write about a glorious eagle or hawk. A buzzard came and told me that we would have a pretty ugly world if they did not clean up. The buzzard made it into the book."

Well, she was put in her place! There is no room for prejudice in the animal kingdom. So you must embrace the animal who comes to you—whatever species!

At any rate, if you plan to understand the world of animal communications you really should know who your animal guide is. I will teach you my personal method of visualizing this (adapted from Anita's exercise), explain a few variations, give you a step by step guide—and then I will introduce you to my animal spirit guides, so you can understand where all the stories in this book really come from.

Creative Visualization

I like to think that my own personal visualization leading to my animal spirits is unique—and, quite frankly, fun. I've explored my inner mind and have come up with a theme that fits a variety of uses for me. I just expanded it to include my animals. Whether it's animal communications I seek, or religious understanding, self-exploration, calming stress factors, or any other number of needs that hit me during the day or night, this "place" in my visualized world fits me well. Locating that place is often practiced in meditation, yoga, stress-release methods, and for self-hypnosis (stop smoking, stop

eating, stop fearing crowds, healing yourself, etc.). In other words, it's well known and used by many. The brand you use is your choice. You can dream it up right in your brain.

Finding myself a fan of science fiction (Does that surprise you? Thought not!), I have taken the stance that if you can get to it all in one place under one guise, rather than having varied themes, it's that much less for you to think about as you try to enter into that realm that is your mind. I use an elevator. It goes up. It goes down. And it stops on floors that have the feel of *Star Trek*'s *hollodeck*. That is, for those of you who do not favor this forever television show, my elevator doors open onto many different scenes that I might require to relax and immerse myself into as I move into the world beyond my living room.

As in hypnosis, I use a counting method to begin. Some people need to use a long counting regiment—your elevator (or staircase, or whatever motion movement you choose) can have as many floors or layers as you need. I only need four—some people may need 104. I start on floor four and then go down into my subconscious by taking the elevator down. Each floor on the way down or up (as my needs dictate) takes me to a place suited especially for my desires at that moment.

My animal communications "place" can be found on the ground level of my elevator. This is not a lone animal place, however. As my elevator doors open on the ground level, they open to a warm nighttime beach. At either side, as I step out, are buildings—one structure to the right holds the past, the other on the left leads to the future. There are times when I use this level to explore questions relating to past and future events of my own personal life. At those times, I will enter the buildings. In future's building, I will often find plastic or drape cloths scattered about showing a part of the house under construction or renovations. I will step over obstacles, duck beneath tarps. It is difficult to manipulate this building for it tells of things that might be—or not. In the building of the past, there are well-decorated rooms, leading me to recall places I've been, decisions I've made. Though

these rooms are not difficult to maneuver, they may have stuck or locked doors or signs that tell me that my remembrances may cause pain. For animal communications, I ignore these buildings and move out further into the ground-floor scene.

There, of course, is the beach beyond, warm breeze on the wind, soft lapping sounds of the

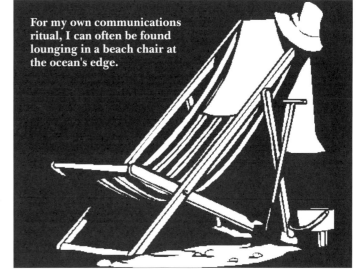

For my own communications ritual, I can often be found lounging in a beach chair at the ocean's edge.

29

water on the sands. A large beach blanket is there with any number of lawn chairs centered on the blanket. If I need "alone time" to think, there is one chair. If I need to speak to my spirit guides, angels, or other religious figures, there are more chairs. Each is facing out towards the water. As you can probably guess, this, too is not the place of animal communications, though my animal guides sometimes visit with me there to watch the water. It's a great way to get to sleep at night.

Just prior to the beach, there is a path off to the left and my scene changes. There is a forest at the path's end, with trees tall and green—trees like you see in Oregon that go up and up forever. This is the place of my animal spirit guides.

When first learning and exploring animal communications, I created an elaborate ritual to get to my guides and to speak to the animals in my life who had issues. This was needed to take my mind down deeper into my subconscious where I could hear clearly and block out the real world. So, at the start of the path to the woods was a beautiful wooden roll-top desk. I would go to the desk, and roll the top up, feeling and hearing the click of each slat as it moved upward. Beneath the slatted aged top was a very large and old book, dressed in worn and soft leather. On the front of the book were pictures of my two animal spirit guides—yes, I have two, but I'll get to that when I teach you how to find yours! I would silently acknowledge them by thanking them for being there for me this day and hoped that they would help me locate a particular animal. Then, I would open the pages of the book. The place I randomly turned to in the book would show the photograph of the animal I sought (already provided to me by the human owning that particular animal)—I move the physical photo into my mind's eye, which in this case, is the book. I would study the animal for a moment, close the book, and then head down the path.

By the time I was at the edge of the woods, my animal spirit guides would be there waiting for me. And they would have the animal I needed to talk to with them. The communication would begin.

Once the communication was over, I would thank the animal and my guides and walk back to the beach. This, then, was when I could return to my physical state and relate what I'd learned about the animal in question.

I found, though, shortly after I began this ritual, that my subconscious became sharper and I no longer needed to go down the path nor look into the book. In fact, as soon as the elevator doors opened on the ground floor, the animal in question would be at the opening with my animal spirit guides to greet me. As time went on, an entire entourage—actually a core group as I began to call them—of my animal clients would be there for my support, creating a line or half circle as the elevator doors opened.

Because this method has been so helpful to me, this is the one I will use to both help you identify your spirit animal and to open up your communications link with your own animal. Or if you've only an interest in what I do and not doing this yourself, you can use this method for stress management, self-exploration, or any spiritual discipline you prefer.

If you hate the idea, feel free to skip to Chapter Two (but you'll be sorry and will probably end up back here anyway!).

Now Visualize

I'm going to ask that you visualize this as you read it. Instead of skimming or just reading through this short exercise. Stop at each paragraph and picture in your mind the things I am telling you. Relax as you do this. This is important, because the first time you carry out this exercise, you will learn who your spirit animal is. Sometimes, the exciting effect is lost if you go back to try it later. If you don't plan to take about fifteen minutes of quiet time to do it correctly, now, please skip this part for the moment and move to *The Learning Curve* on the next pages. The first communications with your guide is important and you don't want your mind to be jaded.

Once you find your animal, you can then use this visualization for any point of reference. **But do be vigilant this first time.**

Find a comfortable, quiet spot where you will not be disturbed. You may sit or recline as you choose— just don't become comfortable enough to fall asleep. I prefer sitting for that very reason. Relax your limbs and take deep breaths.

Imagine that you are on an elevator. You have entered at the 4th floor level. You are alone on this elevator and the space is comfortably conditioned (warm or cool) as your needs require at this moment. (Breath deeply.) You can look up and see the floor numbers clearly shown on the digital display overtop the elevator door. You can see the buttons on the side door panel where you will choose the floor you will visit. You note the reflective walls of the elevator— either mirror like, wood grain, or any other pleasing combination of materials. You push the G (ground floor level) on the door panel. You lean against the back wall, feeling the cool surface against your back and watch the floor indicator as it moves slowly downward. This elevator moves a tad bit slower than a normal elevator, and you can consciously feel that movement in your stomach telling you that you are going down.

You watch the digital display move from 4 to 3. Breathe deeply, release any other thoughts you might have, except the number shown on the elevator display. Concentrate on the number. The elevator will not move downward until you see only the number and no other thoughts are intruding.

You watch the digital display move from 3 to 2. Breathe deeply. Release intruding thoughts. Watch only the number display.

You watch the digital display move from 2 to 1. Breathe deeply.

You watch the digital display move from 1 to G (ground). Breathe deeply.

The elevator doors open and you feel the warm comfortable nighttime air of a beach scene flow in. You step out onto warm sand. In the distance, you can hear the water slap against the shore. The moon is full and sheds glistening white light all around you.

You follow the sand towards the beach. At a point along the path, you see another pathway to your left. You choose to take it. Oddly, as you start down this path, the nighttime light changes to sunshine. This does not bother you and you consciously feel the warm sunlight on your skin. It feels luscious! The nature around you is beautiful. Color surrounds you. There are flowers and trees and all manner of nature sounds. You stop a moment to take it all in, looking at trees and flowers as you welcome the beauty of each.

After a few moments of appreciating this natural scene, you begin to walk again and stop just short of the wooded forest. You note that the forest is thick and appears to be a cool retreat on a warm summer morning. The tall trees reach high up to a blue sky and a gentle breeze touches your skin. You do not enter the forest. Rather, you look into the wooded area, trying to see beyond the soaring tree lines.

Spirit sometimes can confuse you. A perfect example might be when they tell you that an animal guide is a camel, but it's really an ostrich.

For you see, you can hear the sound of movement coming from inside the forest, moving toward you. It's a welcoming sound, one that makes you eager and excited. Someone is coming to greet you! You hear the rustling of the foliage on the ground. You hear the movement coming closer and closer. Soon, you will be able to see who it is!

And now, an animal bursts through the edge of the woods to the path in front of you! What animal do you see?

The first animal that pops into your mind will be your spirit animal. You will see the animal clearly as it comes out of the wooded forest. Or you may see the words printed on your mind. Sometimes, you just "know." Other times you may *feel* the identity.

The Learning Curve

There is something else I've learned while attempting to teach others how to conduct this visualization. Most people forget when they are teaching something—unless they are very used to adult education training—that people learn in different ways. They also "visualize" in different ways. This often means without visual depth! A bit later in my book, you will meet Mary Gasparo, a ghost hunter who, until just recently, did not understand that she was empathic. She *felt* things. She did not *see* them. So, as I was taking her through the exercise, she was trying not to show disappointment and discouragement—you see, she couldn't see my elevator…or the fields, or the path, or the desk. And she couldn't even *see* her animal.

I was surprised and didn't know what to make of it at first until she told me that she could, however, smell the flowers and feel the sunshine on her face. She also *felt* her animal and thought that she knew what it was in that way. That's when we both realized that she didn't "visualize"—she felt things. And she could also smell things. This was a breakthrough not only with animal communications, but for her in her ghost hunting.

I tell you this to say that not everyone gathers information in the same way. Be aware of that and not hard on yourself if your "visualization" feels, looks, smells, or *is* different than mine. By the way, I suppose it's as good a time as any to advise you that the images you get, at this point,

In reality, the ostrich is known as Struthio camelus (struthio meaning *ostrich* and camelus meaning *camel*). I certainly felt silly not knowing that!

35

and when you are communicating with animals can be a bit confusing. Before I took Mary through her visualization exercise, I asked my own spirit animal guides what Mary's animal would be. I wrote it on a piece of paper and filed it away in my purse. The animal I was given and the one I wrote down was "Camel." I'd planned to take her through a full camel exercise once she'd discovered that the camel was her guide.

But the animal she felt turned out not to be a camel. I was shocked, not expecting to be wrong. She'd felt an ostrich. I couldn't believe how far off I was. Doubts of my abilities again plagued me.

Once home, though, I looked up the ostrich online and found a surprise. The technical scientific name for the ostrich is: *Struthio camelus (struthio* meaning ostrich and *camelus* meaning camel). Now why the guides couldn't just tell me ostrich, I haven't a clue. This was incredibly irritating! But it does show that what you get, may not always be exactly as things are—thus the mysteries that one must wade through. This stuff *ain't* easy sometimes! But it keeps you on your toes!

Getting to Know Your Spirit Animal

You may be very surprised at the animal that has chosen to help you communicate—or, it may be a presence that is familiar to you. But whether familiar or not, you may find certain senses, unfelt or unnoticed before, are coming to you frequently and persistently once you open your awareness. For example, I can often feel my animal spirit guides (and my regular guides) with an electrical sensation touching the left side of my body. The feeling is strong enough now that I always stop whatever I'm doing to listen to my subconscious mind. That first thought transmitted to me is most often from spirit. Feelings on the left side of the body, I've found, seem to be from spirit—a connection. Though I must admit that some of the electrical sensations during my ghost investigations have also occurred on the left side, too. I can also tell spirit, of one kind or another, is around me

I feel a heaviness (often confused with dizziness, sinus pressure, or disorientation) on the top of my head. This is the opening of the crown chakra which is one's connection to the universe, the world as a whole, and the energies that are drawn into the soul. And, oftentimes, there will be a chilling of the air. These things happen when you practice interacting with spirit.

I do need to clarify here. The sensations I've just mentioned are not those felt during mediation to contact your guides; rather they are feelings that arise when the guides are attempting to contact you—at least in my experience. This is most often the case when you are doing something entirely unrelated to seeking them. For example, I might be typing at my computer and my right side will begin to tingle. I stop because I know there's a message. I hadn't sought one—but they had one for me. The very thought in my head at that moment of the sensation, usually appearing in my own thought patterns, is spirit.

An example of this, so that you understand how closely oriented you and your guides are, would be like this example: I was editing a book early in the morning at the office at a time when only I was there. My office is situated back away from most of the office hub

The chakras of the body are great indicators of spiritual matters. The crown chakra, for example, links you to the universe.

and I rarely notice things happening outside it, even when there *are* others around. I was very "into" what I was doing this particular morning. Suddenly, the tingle sensation hit the left side of my body. I stopped editing immediately. The thought popped into my mind. *Someone else has arrived.* Seconds later, one of my coworkers popped her head into my office; she was an early worker as well on that day. It was an inconsequential thing, but had I not been made aware of the presence, I would have jumped when she came into my office. My guides were considerate enough not to let that happen with a quick "warning." Now *these* guides watching over me throughout the day are my "regular" guides, not the animal companions. The animal guides only stay close when I'm in need of animal-related communications or advice.

On that first day in Anita's seminar, I learned that I, personally, had two animal guides. My communications guide was a leopard—named quite appropriately Leo. Let me take a moment here to tell you that though your guides will provide you with names if you ask, these are only a consideration for you as a human. Spirits do not need names, but since we identify our internal images with names and figures, they accommodate us. When I met Leo on the path to the forest during my first session, I took time to walk with him in the woods and to feel his strength. Additionally, Anita had her students move their own bodies and consciousnesses into their animals to feel what it would be like to "wear" the animal. So I found myself inside the leopard, one with the creature, roaming the forest and being part of all the sensations a leopard would feel as he prowled his domain.

Interestingly enough, a lemur was also in attendance. This funny and agile creature identified himself as Lee, my regular animal guide who had been with me all my life. I'd met him already, years prior. His wide eyes and jovial nature enveloped me in a giddy fashion. Mixing the two personalities of my animal guides, I found that I could look at the serious side of the animal world as well as the lighthearted side. The combination of spirit was perfect for me.

So now, after being closely attached to these animals in spirit, I find them everywhere in my visualizations. They stay together, the lemur often riding the leopard, as they supervise and advise

during my animal communication rituals. No matter how quickly I fall into my interactions with the animals, these two magnificent beings are there. I've come to rely on them.

And I must tell you that guides in general have great senses of humor and mine often cackle at my expense. As I was looking through my notes from my very first encounter in Anita's class, I found a notation that I'd overlooked before because it made no sense at the time and … well, for whatever reason, I'd just shrugged it off.

I wrote in my notes:

> *Leopard and lemur have a message for Carroll [my husband]. The check is in the mail—laugh/ giggle—or under the hutch. [More laughing.]*

At the time and up until this point, I had no clue what that meant. Then, today (months

There is plenty of room beneath this hutch for one to look to find a missing check. There's no mistaking the area for empty one minute and the check there the next!

later), as I type this manuscript using my notes for inspiration, I see the significance! Carroll's mom had given him a present in the form of a check. He'd laid it on the countertop of the hutch. The next day it was gone. We looked *everywhere* for it. We searched on top the hutch, under it, around it, the trash can, every conceivable place in the house. My husband was furious at this disappearance. But I had an inkling that it was spirit playing games (or ghosts—remember I'm a ghost hunter and this is something that often happens with ghosts. They love to take things.).

I told him to just let it go, and in a day or two, it would turn up where we least expected it. This had happened to me before with spirit. He didn't believe me, and stayed obsessed for quite some time, but there was nothing else to do. The check was gone. Two days later, we were sitting on the couch, facing the hutch, and I could see a paper under it on the hardwood floor. Mind you, we'd both looked there before on hands and knees and the check had not been there.

Yes. It was the check. I knew then that it was spirit, but now I see that I was also warned about losing the check *before* it was ever lost! In addition to a sense of humor, this may also give a foreshadowing of how time as we know it is absent on the otherside.

Know that *your* guides, whether serious or funny, are there for *you* as well. You don't have to acknowledge them if that is not your interest in this book. It matters not, they are there and they are casually by your side, waiting for you to invite them into your lives. They never leave. It is my suggestion that you relish their friendship and get to know them. Great times are in store for you if you do.

2. The One, the Only, the Great — Bentley

"Typically, something only goes after and tests those who it feels are a direct threat or someone who is going to be directly involved with the investigation."

~Kim Ritchie, Ghost Investigator

Bentley, as I've said early on, was a bird with attitude. But, at first, I didn't know that. In fact, I felt that my sanity was in question when it came to this whole chatting with the bird thing. I sat at my computer gazing at the photo that author Marla Brooks had sent to me showing the pretty bird. Only in my mind, I didn't see this bird at all. I saw the bird from the television show from years and years ago, entitled *Baretta*. It was a private eye detective show (if I recall correctly) with the head detective having a lovely white bird—a bird with an attitude. This bird was a major part of the show as it depicted the characters' personalities and helped the slant of the series. However, what did this bird have to do with Marla's bird, Bentley? Why was I seeing it in my mind?

There was a bigger problem in the scheme of things. Just what was I supposed to say to Marla? While it was true that we'd grown to be friends through the process of publishing a book or two, and she was very amenable to my quirky personality, what would she think if I told her that I thought her bird was a private detective? Or at least that *he* thought he was. And that he was in charge and the only one *in the know* about anything that had value. We were talking about a bird, for heaven sakes!

But who knew just how much of a detective this little guy was…

Go to Hell…

As I began that first journey to talk with Bentley, I went through my full ritual, finding myself at the forest with my spirit guides, Lee the Lemur and Leo the Leopard. The Lemur was perched atop the Leopard's back.

"I'm not doin' this one," said the Lemur, a brand of irritation in his voice that I'd not heard before. He then jumped off the leopard's back.

Bentley is quite the photogenic fellow, knowing that he is the prettiest bird of all birds. *Photo courtesy of Marla Brooks.*

The leopard replied, "She [meaning Marla] said the bird was crotchety."

"I don't care; I'm not doin' it," said the Lemur and he moved away.

It was then that the leopard looked up, strolling along with me following. "The bird's already here," he said.

42

Indeed he was. He was a little thing standing next to the magnificent leopard, but you could tell right away that he would've taken on the leopard in a battle to the death (probably his) in a heartbeat should he be angered.

"Hello there," I said to Bentley, "I'm—

"Go to Hell; you don't know nothin'."

Marla Brooks is the renowned author of the *Ghosts of Hollywood* **series. And boy does she have a haunted house!** *Photo courtesy of Marla Brooks.*

It was a statement. A harsh statement. A statement that was meant to throw fear into my heart—or at the very least, to surprise me and send me packing. How could I answer such a thing?

I shook my head. It was certain that I was a nutcase. These impressions and thoughts hit me like a bus filled with squawking birds in the seconds it took Bentley to tell me to, "Go to Hell."

I was shocked and immediately questioned what I was hearing. This had to be my mind. I was making it up as part of some bird folly fantasy that had been secluded in the back of my warped mind waiting to spring forth from oblivion. *What? I have a bird fantasy?* Well it had to be something like that, cuz birds didn't tell people to *go to hell*. Unless, taught to, anyway. And if all this was true, then I had definitely gone over the deep end.

My mind's eye showed the caricature of this bird (who now *did* look like the bird in Bentley's picture) tapping his little foot in agitation and angry as a snake. It was as though he was daring me to say another word, and if I did, he was there to make me sorry for it. Maybe peck my eyes out or poop

43

on my head. And somehow, I knew he was the one bird who could do it, too. *Can psychiatrists help people like me?* I thought quickly.

I tried again. "Bentley, I am—"

"Go to hell. I'm not talkin' to you," he said.

I looked to the leopard and I swear if a leopard could shrug, he did.

I forced the issue with Bentley. "But I wanted to talk with you for Marla, your mom—"

"Go to hell; I got nothin' to say to you; you don't know nothin'."

"I don't disagree," I said. Then I got the feeling again—the *knowing*—about the TV bird and knew that this bird thought he was a private detective of sorts and that he had major importance in his household. In charge. No nonsense. The boss. Nose in everything.

"Let me just give a message to her from you," I pleaded. "Just one message. Then I'll go away."

Then, as quick as a response as I could have asked for, he said, "Tell her to fix the dam perch."

I replied, "What's wrong with your perch?"

"It hurts my feet." (Could birds growl? Darned if I didn't get that impression.)

"Is it broken?" I inquired.

It felt as though he was rolling his eyes—even though I know birds don't do that—uhmm, *can't* do that. "No, it's old and worn. Don't I deserve to have a new one?" (This was said in a not-so-nice, old man, crotchety-type manner. Bentley was anything but polite.)

"Go to hell, I got nothin' to say. I'm not talkin' to you no more," he said.

And he was gone. My mind was blank.

I started gently. "Marla, I'm seeing that bird from the television show *Baretta*."

44

She replied, "No…Bentley doesn't look anything like that bird—that bird's a cockatoo and Bentley's a cocka*tiel*."

So far so good. She wasn't laughing yet. I began again. "Well, it's not so much that particular bird…rather that bird's attitude…kinda cocky…in charge…and Bentley was…well, mean and kinda nasty. He told me to *go to hell*." I held my breath.

Now she was laughing. (Was it at me or what I said? I didn't know what was so funny!) "That sounds just like him! He's a crotchety old man!"

Marla told me that Bentley had been with her for nearly twenty-five years; they'd been through thick and thin and he'd always been her buddy. There was a real relationship there. She said, "He's a true character who thinks very highly of himself and can often be found walking back and forth in front of the mirror wolf whistling at his own reflection. Several times during the day, he breaks into song and serenades us with "Yankee Doodle" and "Beethoven's Fifth Symphony." She went on to tell me that he preferred whistling to talking, though he did say "Hello" to her in the morning when she first uncovered his cage.

Not to say that she'd not been exposed to the crotchety behavior a time or two. Bentley was old for his kind, and he was pretty darn moody a lot of the time. In fact, there were times when he took out his frustrations on Marla by flying into her head and pecking at her or nipping her on the earlobe. And he was none too gentle at those times. This boy was a character and a half.

Marla told me that, oddly, she'd been thinking about changing his perch, since he'd been standing on the same one for many years. She was surprised that she'd picked up somehow on his feeling and then had that feeling confirmed by me. But there was more to this whole "talking with the bird" than met the eye.

"I was pretty sure that there was more to what Bentley was feeling then complaining about his perch," she said seriously. In fact, this pretty bird had taken to being afraid of the dark when he'd never had such a propensity before. I listened as

45

she told me about Bentley's rituals. At night, she would cover his cage and he'd be content in that little hideaway until morning. But lately, that has not been the case.

He'd become afraid of the dark.

As soon as she would cover his cage, he would begin pecking at his chest and wings, all the while chirping nervously. (I wondered, as she talked, what could spook this little dynamo. Had to be something pretty big.) She told me that sometimes he pecked so hard that he would knock himself clean off his perch. Had this not been a serious thing, I might have laughed, thinking that it may have served him right. But not this time. I knew something else was going on. I don't know how I knew, but something was not right at the Brooks house.

And Marla was worried. At first she'd thought that maybe he was ill or that he was experiencing a kind of bird senility. But once he was uncovered and she'd turned on the lights, or the sun shone in, he was back to being the old cantankerous Bentley.

Now, if you recall, Marla Brooks is a ghost investigator as well as author. She also has some psychic ability. She is no stranger to the bizarre or to things that go bump in the night. And her hackles were up. It seemed that Bentley now had taken to saying *hello* every so often when nobody was in the room. This was not something he did. He spoke only to her.

The plot thickened.

Only the Shadow Knows

This strange behavior went on for a couple weeks before Marla decided to call me again. She had two other animals in her home, Pipsqueak the cat, and Kalli the dog, and not only did she want to check in on them, but she wanted another reading with Bentley. Things were not good on the homefront with the grumpy bird. Not only was he demanding to be in lamp light all night long (which plays havoc on a human's nighttime sleeping habits), but he was pecking himself to pieces. He was a wreck and reducing everyone else around him to emotional rubble.

I settled myself down and instructed Marla to be very quiet while I tuned into the bird, and only to respond when I asked her specific questions. I went through my ritual and very quickly saw the little bird in my mind's eye looking back at me. Only this time, Bentley was not abusive. In fact, he was quick to engage, which let me know right away that he was pretty upset about something. So after saying hello and having him wave away the niceties—as if to tell me to get on with it already; there were mysteries to be solved—I asked him why he was chewing himself.

Before he could answer me, I saw something else—and it startled me. It was a shadow. And not a pleasant one. It was a billowing kind of thing, dark and moving. This was totally unexpected, because it was not an animal thing; it was a ghost thing. Telling Marla immediately what I saw, she did not seem surprised. She asked *where*.

Without Bentley telling me, I saw the thing in my mind hovering in the corner of the room—it filled the corner and had dark blacks, grays, and whites swirling in it. This was an empty corner in her home and the shadow, of human height, did not reach all the way to the floor. At this point, I didn't know what amazed me more—the fact that I could contact Bentley or that I could actually see the shadow. (Another new skill on the forefront?)

I turned my attention back to the bird, who though waiting, was not patient. I could tell somehow that Bentley was not exactly *afraid* of the shadow, but he was disturbed by it because it was in what he felt was his space. It made him very uncomfortable and he wanted it to go away. His nerves were on edge. My heart went out to the little fellow. He'd lived a comfortable long life with a doting mama in Marla, and now, after all those years, there was a dark shadow on the scene.

Marla was pensive for only a moment before telling me how creeped out she was by all this because just a few days before, Ken (who is a partner in Marla's household) described a big shadowy figure dart into her bedroom. "It was really big, and definitely male,"

Ken had said. And he'd also told her that he could see it more clearly than any of the other spirits that he'd seen at the house. Marla has a slew of ghostly guests that come and go in her Hollywood home. But we'll get to that later. My questions were: What was this thing? Why was it there?

Bentley could care less. He just wanted it gone.

The night Ken saw the figure fly into the bedroom, where Bentley's cage resides, was the night that our fine-feathered friend began pecking at himself as soon as the lights went out. Having so much paranormal activity in the home on a regular basis, Marla had not connected the incidents to her bird's behavior.

Marla did the best she could for the short term, leaving Bentley's cage uncovered at night and keeping a night light on for him. Though that seemed to help, she was determined to get to the bottom of this shadow mystery and not just put a Band-Aid® light on the whole matter. She came to me again, hoping that if I talked to her sweet little cat, Pipsqueak, and her rambunctious dog, Kalli, maybe they could shed light on things that she and Ken were not aware of.

Pipsqueak was of particular interest because she had changed her routine—which was not routine.

Pipsqueak is a prominent member of the Brooks household. When her routine changes, however, it's something to keep an eye on. Something was definitely afoot in the bedroom. *Photo courtesy of Marla Brooks.*

Usually, the kitty spent her time in the bedroom sleeping on the bed, but since the strange shadow had arrived on the scene, she'd been hanging out under Marla's desk in her office, adjacent to the bedroom, where she could be close to Marla. This was odd behavior indeed.

So I set up a time to check in with the lovely Pipsqueek. It's funny how the things people think would upset animals and what the real story is may be completely different. I think that we often project our own feelings onto our partner creatures. At any rate, Pips told me that not only was she fine, but that she saw shadows in their home all the time. They were "no big deal." The problem, or caution, now was that Bentley was uncomfortable and noticing something when he normally did not care about anything. This had put her on alert. If Bentley thought there was a problem, well, there must be a problem. She felt that this particular shadow warranted attention and that the best place for her during this time was close to her mom—under the desk, securely at Marla's feet. A safe place to watch

from. She told me that Bentley usually had a good take on things, and that if he was nervous enough to peck himself, maybe she should think about the situation more.

(She also wanted to tell me that Bentley pooped on something of hers and she'd prefer that he not do that again. I couldn't make out what that something was, but it brought a giggle to my heart.)

I decided to check in with Kalli as well, but at this time, Kalli couldn't be bothered with things such as shadows. It was nonsense, but she had decided to allow Pips to check things out just in case. The dog thought the bird had "issues" beyond the shadow incidents anyway. I got a distinct yawn in my sixth sense to show me how much of a bore this was for Kalli.

After Marla and Ken heard what I had to say, they thought it might be a good idea to find out who or what, if possible, this shadow was and then to make it go away. Despite the animals' odd discomfort about the anomaly, Marla did not feel that this "thing" was really malevolent, but she didn't want Bentley pecking himself to death either. So she called on her spirit guides to escort the shadow away. That night, she was able to cover Bentley's cage and he slept well. But the incident was far from over.

Kalli had more worries than a mere shadow to think about. *Photo courtesy of Marla Brooks.*

The Shadow Persists

It wasn't long before Bentley started pecking himself again. I suppose that even our guides sometimes have trouble keeping interlopers or trespassers away if they are persistent enough. It was time to talk with the bird again.

This time my animal guides hung back a bit and allowed me to do the calling. It wasn't that they didn't like the sometimes condescending Bentley, but I do think that his abrasive attitude was at times more than they cared to swallow. They stood to one side of me as I talked to the bird, who materialized immediately when I called him and stepped right up as though we'd been the best of friends forever and a day. Still, I was wary. This was a contrary one.

"Bentley, I know you don't like talking to me, but you are so beautiful and you're pecking yourself again. Marla is worried about you." I was hoping that a bit of bird schmoozing might turn his head—or at least keep him from telling me to go to hell.

But he wasn't mean this time. He simply hung his little head and said, "I know, I know." This showed me how much he loved Marla and possibly that he was worried about himself as well.

"What's going on?" I asked gently.

"You already know. It's the shadow. It's still here."

I'd told him in a prior session that he should not let this strange shadow worry him, that Marla would be there to protect him. I reminded him, "But I told you that you were protected by your mom."

"Yes, but it's still here and it smirks at me. I don't like that. It needs to go away."

There was an edge to his tone this time. The shadow had stepped over that invisible line. Yes, it had worried him enough to make him peck at himself, but now, it had done the unthinkable. It had smirked. *No* one laughed at this no-nonsense bird. I had the feeling he would make it pay, if he could.

But there was still a problem. The shadow had come back even though ushered away by very-powerful spirit guides. This surprised me, but I still tried to ease Bentley's unease.

"Do you understand that sometimes, it's not that easy to make something go when we don't understand it?"

He wasn't having any of it, though. "What's to understand? It's a shadow. Make it go."

"Do you know how to make it go?" I asked, because sometimes we underestimate how much our animals can actually do or understand.

"You people are supposed to know how to do that." Apparently, Bentley didn't know how to make it go.

"It's not that easy, but I do tell you that you are protected and that you shouldn't let it annoy you or pay any attention to it smirking." I tried the advice that was used for bullies in the human world. If they don't think what they do to you upsets you, they usually give up and go away. I swallowed hard, though, because I also knew that ignoring bullies could sometimes incite more intense bullying. I hoped with fervor that this was not the case for Bentley and the shadow intruder.

"Easy for you to say. Look, just make it go away." He seemed to be imploring me now and I felt bad that I couldn't just wave a magic wand for him to get rid of this trespasser.

What else might work, I wondered. "Do you want Marla to move your cage?"

He'd been relatively calm up until this point, but I was trying his patience. The old Bentley came back. "What, hey, am I talkin' to myself here? Make the *shadow* go away. Not *me*." Then, as if by magic, Kalli and Pips were

there and Bentley was directing my attention to them. He said, "The big furball knows how to make it go."

"You mean Kalli or Pips?" I asked, trying to make sure whether it was the cat or the dog he was talking about.

"It doesn't like their kind—cats. The one is trying, but both of 'em need to chase it out. That other one doesn't care about me." I was becoming confused. Was he talking about Pips? Did she not like him? That hadn't been the impression I'd gotten when talking to her earlier.

"Are you saying that the cat should hang out where the shadow has been seen? And that it doesn't like cats? And that Pips doesn't like you."

But he went on without answering me, as if he was in a dialog all his own. "It doesn't care for me either, but I don't bother it. It smirks—even when I talk to it. I know I shouldn't talk to it but how else will she know it's around at other times?" Ah, the "she" this time was Marla. Bentley was giving signals to Marla when the shadow was around by talking to it.

I tried again to pull him back to my train of thought. "Marla has trouble sleeping with the light on and is worried about you pecking your pretty self."

"Then...get...rid...of...the...thing. Nothing was done to get rid of it." He was strongly agitated now. "I got nothing more to say, I told you that before. Just make it go. Get the furballs on it."

Bentley's reference to "cats" (plural furballs) kind of took me by surprise because there was only one cat in residence, though I found out later that there once had been four. Old age and infirmity took the other three over the past few years. Could Bentley have seen a cat spirit as well and not known the difference between the living and the dead? I'd had experiences with other animals that indicated that very thing.

I assured Bentley that I'd talked to Marla and that not only would I ask Pipsqueak for help to get the shadow person out, but that his mom would be trying to banish it as well.

Unfortunately, though, even though I had the best of intentions and Marla was doing everything she could think of to get rid of the pesky shadow, Bentley was back to fearing the dark and pecking himself whenever the lights went out.

Marla, if nothing but ingenious, called in the big guns. After all, Bentley was a family member in trouble and something had to be done. She called up a friend psychic, Lisa J. Smith, an intuitive healer/medium/energy reader with a direct link to the spirit world. A part of the CBS radio Show, *PsychicRadio*, Lisa is well-known for her honesty and passion for helping others through their rough spots of spiritualism. Marla hoped that Lisa might be able to tune into the shadow to find out who or what it was.

Barely had Marla gotten the question out of her mouth when Lisa replied that the uninvited guest was a man by the name of Frank.

Frank From the Bank

I should mention here that Marla Brooks wears many hats. Not only is she a travel writer, master chef (though I haven't had the chance to sample—hint, hint, Marla), bewitching witch and spell caster, and premier animal lover, she is also, as I have mentioned, the ghost hunter of choice in Hollywood. There are not many ghosts in Tinseltown that haven't had the pleasure of her investigations and she's forever solving one phantom mystery after another.

But sometimes, investigations don't go exactly as planned. Things go on in the world on the other side where we haven't any knowledge. It's almost as if those spirits whisper behind our backs, coming up with creative ways to get our attention. They hide our keys only to put them back in strange locations; they walk our floors leaving telltale sounds of footsteps in our ears. I could go on and on about the things that ghosts do or don't do.

The haunted bank vault at the Bank of American building in Hollywood, California. Orbs found here are most likely connected to the mob. *Photo courtesy of Marla Brooks.*

I, however, digress. The bank. And Frank. The Bank of America building—known by other names, as well—located at the corner of Hollywood and Highland in Hollywood, California, is haunted. It's a bank with lots of interesting history, the most attention-grabbing being as a jumping-off point for Superman in the old '50s television series. (For a bird story, there has to be a flying connection, right? Why not *Superman*? Bentley would approve.) Of course, there were the normal haunting-type things going on there: footsteps, door slamming, voices when no one was there. But there were other things, more distressing things, that went on as well.

Marla took a team in to explore. Comprised of a psychic, a historical researcher, a photographer, and another sensitive, the team was there to investigate the bank for her *Ghosts of Hollywood II* book. From the things she'd heard, she wasn't taking chances. This was the night to find out the real scoop behind the paranormal activity in this most exciting building.

Though I could go into depth about the kinds of things they found, let me summarize just so you see how important the connection between the bank and Bentley was. People had been killed during the 1930 heydays here, and there were brawls aplenty—probably from illegitimate money activities, Mafia, and speakeasies. The place was filled to the brim with ghosts going about their daily activities amongst the four living investigators. Money laundering, rape, murder, frightening stuff.

So, of course, the ghost hunting group would conduct a séance. I don't know whether I say that in sarcasm or in true investigative form. I just know that this is where everything began. Poor Bentley. Picture, if you will, a séance table sitting in the middle of a …wait for it… bank vault (I never said Marla wasn't crazed!). Lights out with the vault lit only by candlelight. On the table sits a Ouija board. Not being novices, the group prepared by saying the right prayers to protect themselves during this endeavor. Note: Never use a Ouija board without conducting the proper preparation rituals, and then still think twice. This can be a dangerous tool for those not in the know.

The psychic on board this evening was Victoria Gross, author of *Ghosts of Orange County*, psychic, and professional Tarot reader. She felt a presence immediately as they began their session. A man involved with illegal activities in the basement area, where the vault is located, was there with them—he'd witnessed something horrible and had been tortured and killed for it. They asked him to spell his name on the Ouija board. (You got it.) F. R. A. N. K. Victoria went on to say that he was a big man and seemed to be in charge of the other spirits in the basement. She felt that he coexists with us—only he is physically in a different dimension.

The evening went on with more mysteries unveiled, but as things were coming to a close, Marla made a mistake. It wasn't a bad mistake. And it wasn't something that any good ghost hunter worth his or her salt would not have done. I've personally done this. But for her—and for Bentley—this time, it was a mistake with grave repercussions. She'd asked for a final sign. With her tape recorder running:

> "…I called out and asked the entities if they would please give us all a sign of their presence before we left the basement…a kind of 'one for the road' experience for us…"

Knowing the end result, I can feel that you, too, may be cringing as you read this.

Well, nothing happened and Marla was disappointed. As she arrived home and the group was standing in front of her home, she heard a loud voice. Eventually, looking around and then listening closely, she realized that her tape recorder had forwarded itself and was now playing back her enticement of the spirits to give them a sign. It was her own voice.

But Marla had rewound the tape prior to leaving the site all the way to the beginning—now it was playing a specific part that occurred much later on the tape.

Her words:

"Even though I was disappointed that the spirits didn't comply with my request to make their presence known as we left the bank building, apparently someone must've heard me, followed us home, and decided to give us a belated surprise. It was quite unnerving, but better late than never."

Then she opened the door to her home. Presto bingo, Frank.

In later research, she found that a man named Frank DeSimone was a crime boss for the Los Angeles Mafia from 1957 to 1967. Now I'm not saying that *this* Frank is *our* Frank…but you do the math.

Now, maybe the mystery of who the shadow is has been solved (or not), but another fact remains that is not so easily sighed away. Bentley is still afraid of the dark and Marla is forced to sleep with the lights on or have one naked bird on her hands.

Hiya Frank!

Bentley was doing his best to let those of us around him know that the situation was not over and that he was not a happy camping bird. One way was by *telling* us. As I mentioned, Bentley doesn't do a lot of "people-talk" in the real world. He says "hello" to Marla first thing in the morning when he sees her get up and he sings a song or two. Mostly, he's a squawker. And I mean that in a good way—thought I'd better say that, cuz he's in my head a lot and I don't like to hear loud angry shrieking.

Our bird hero took to saying hello to something in the bedroom while Marla was occupied elsewhere. She will hear him uncharacteristically greeting "no one." This unnerved her because, in over twenty years, this was not something that Bentley did. He said hello in the morning, to her only, and that was the end of the hello-ing for the day. He was picky about who he addressed (how well I knew that). But he *was* talking to *someone*. This was what he had told me in our prior session. "It smirks—even when I talk to it. I know I shouldn't talk to it, but how else will she know it's around at other times?"

At present, I've taught Marla how to give messages to Bentley and she routinely tells him that she is there to protect him. Some days are better than others.

Has the shadow left? I think it must come and go, because there are still spurts of pecking activity in Bentley's behavior. And more than once, Bentley has popped into my life at strange times and places to give me a nasty squawk about not doing something right as far as the shadow goes. Marla has had people in to "clear" her place of negative spirits, has performed spells, and sent the other animals loose in there to rush the shadow out. If it's really a Mafia guy, I don't think they are too easy to dominate…

For example, one morning in the shower, all of a sudden Bentley jumped into my head. This surprised me because I'd never had an animal intrude uninvited.

He was telling me to *Shhhh*.

He said, "It gets power from loud voices."

The bird went on to tell me, as I shampooed, that the shadow doesn't really take notice of him or the other animals, but it stays around. Bentley said that he could see it better at night. I reminded him that he was protected and he agreed that he felt protected by Marla, but then added, "but *he's* not." I believe he meant Marla's roommate, Ken. The bird was still very uncomfortable though, because things could change, and he thought that the shadow might come after *him*.

Bentley seemed to hang his little head when he told me that he'd pecked again the prior night. He forgets not to when he's nervous. It's not that he *wants* to peck, he just forgets, but he did tell me that he would keep an eye on the shadow for his mom.

About the shower visit: From Marla: "It's apropos that Bentley came to you in the shower, because before we remodeled, and I had a stall shower in my bathroom, he LOVED to sit up on the door and get splashed when I took a shower. I know he misses it."

Kalli, though not really interested in the shadow, seems to be frightened of the portal in the front bedroom. Note the orb in this photo...is something already visiting from inside the Portal? *Photo courtesy of Marla Brooks.*

The Portal

Of course, the shadow isn't the only thing going on in the Brooks household that affects the animals living there. Bentley has his shadow and Kalli the dog has the portal in the front bedroom. Marla told me, when we'd first started talking about these things, about her haunted house and neighborhood, and I was very interested, as I am in all hauntings. This was pre-animal communication days, and my mainstay were ghosts in all their glorious manifestations...though I was worried about this haunting from day one.

Wanting to find out who was haunting her house, Marla called in friend and author, psychic Victoria Gross, to get her take on things. Victoria immediately sensed that the northeast corner of the front bedroom was a portal—a gateway for ghosts (or other things) to enter our world from the one beyond. This did not sound good to me. Victoria went on to find many spirits living at the house connected to items and portals in just about all areas of the home. Marla continues to

59

remind me: Never a dull moment concerning ghosts at her house.

It was nearly a year or more after I'd learned about Marla's house that I began talking with Bentley. And though he is star of the shadow story, Kalli is star of the portal story. As I continued to talk to the Brooks animals, usually in Marla's office or bedroom, there was something else that intruded from another area of the house. Bentley was not bothered by it at all, and Pips was such a quiet darling, she never spoke ill of any place or creature—even of shadows and ghosts.

At first, Kalli, too, was oblivious to it all—except when she was actually in the front bedroom. She was bothered by what was there, and often Marla found her behavior to be a bit "off" because of it. I now knew that the dog had seen red eyes peering out of that strange place.

For me, I was beginning to think that I watched too much television. TV shows, *Torchwood* and *Primeval* came to mind as I began to see a green swirling funnel in the corner of the front bedroom reminiscent of a gateway to a world of monsters that one might see in a horror flick. Now this, mind you, when I'd never been to Marla's home and had no psychic ability that I knew of. Marla lives on the other side of the country from me. I'd see this swirling thing every time Marla asked me to talk to Kalli. It had become part of Kalli's baggage to carry around in a way.

It became evident to me that Kalli was frightened of something inside the funnel and was cowering inside

Pipsqueak decides that "telling all" is the best policy when it comes to her own fame in an animal book like this. But is this detrimental to the other animals in the house? Bentley thinks so. *Photo courtesy of Marla Brooks.*

her very soul every time she went into the front bedroom. But there was no keeping her out of the room. She would stay by Ken's side to the end of time—or the world as we know it—for this is where he slept and spent much of his time. She showed me red eyes looking out at her and noticed that sometimes household personalities would flare when something particularly evil stuck its ugly head from the green swirling mass.

Though Kalli was the most affected, the other two animals were not without dealings with the swirling portal. At the point that I began making plans to write this book, I knew that Bentley would be a big part of it because he had been my introduction into animal personality—beyond what I knew about animals from the "normal" perspective. But pensive Pipsqueak did not want to sit in the shadow (forgive the pun) of Bentley. She wanted her own part in the mystery.

And this was her chance.

Star-Struck with the Brooks Animals

Things, though ghostly at the Brooks household, were not always filled with intrigue and fearful goings-on. Marla's animals are quite the characters. Because of all the work I'd done with them, they'd become a special support system as I'd move through my learning stages of animal communications. And they surprise me often. This whole portal incident was a certain shocker.

Bentley was the most out-spoken animal I'd talked with since the very beginning, though you'll meet Solo the horse a bit later. On the day I decided to write this book detailing my journey, Bentley was there jumping around singing *Yankee Doodle Dandy* first thing when I got up that morning. Marla told me that he had squawked her awake in the middle of the night, noting the three-hour time difference between us. He was going to be in a book and he was going to be on the cover and the stories would all be about him. The bird was dancing on air. I couldn't stop laughing. He was such a personality!

On my drive home on a day sometime after learning about the portal, into my mind shot an image of Pipsqueak, accompanied, of course, by the vocal Bentley.

"I can tell you about the portal," said Pips in a very soft and quiet tone. She was a dainty girl and nothing like her companion pet.

"No!" shouted Bentley, who also seemed to materialize out of nowhere. "Don't mention it, don't draw its attention!"

"But I want to be in the book," said Pips, now whining.

"No!" Bentley reiterated. "It's not safe!"

It was time for me to step in—after all, it was my mind these two had bamboozled. "What are you guys talking about?" I asked.

"Pipsqueak wants to be in the book and thinks she has to give up some private information for that to happen," snapped Bentley. "So don't listen to her."

Pipsqueak, however, was ignoring the bird. "It looks out sometimes. Into the room. The thing in the tunnel place."

"No, no! Don't say anymore. You'll draw it's attention and it will see us! We can't have it seeing us!" Bentley was now jumping up and down in bird fashion in my mind.

I didn't really understand what the problem was, but it only took a second or so to put two and two together. Kalli had shown me red eyes earlier, scary eyes that looked out of the portal from time to time. And now these two animals were talking about something looking out at them and letting me know that it was dangerous.

Bentley was addressing me now. "We can't tell you about it, because it may come out after us. We can't talk about it. It doesn't really see us. And we don't want it to. So don't listen to her!"

I could see that the bird was genuinely frightened, but Pips wasn't really telling me something I didn't know. I decided to ease their minds. "You don't have to worry about the book, Pips. You can be in it. You don't have to contribute anything extra to be in it."

All she replied was, "Okay." I felt in my mind a big smile, and she added, "I can be in the book!"

Pipsqueak stands her ground with a very determined personality. *Photo courtesy of Marla Brooks.*

After this talk though, I was truly worried about the portal again. I called Marla to talk to her about it—a warning. She and Ken immediately took extra precautions, but to date, even with psychics coming by to try to alleviate the problem, the portal still seems to exist in their front bedroom and shadows routinely seem to come out of it. They have not seen the red eyes that the animals have seen, but it doesn't surprise them. The negativity in that room is evident from time to time.

I have a feeling that this won't be the last we hear of the portal, either. At this writing, there is still evidence that the portal is open, though Marla has made still more efforts to close it. They keep a close eye on the animals for signs, since they seem to be very affected by the negativity.

After all, a portal goes both ways...

3. Doin' the Good Work — Cooneys

"And before him shall be gathered all nations:
and he shall separate them one from another,
as a shepherd divideth his sheep from the goats".

~Matthew 25:32

Unfortunately, one of the not-so-pleasant things that goes along with being able to communicate with animals has to do with their times of crossing over. Not only is it a stressful time for the animal in some cases—not for the reasons you might think—but feeling the pain of those humans who must leave a fiercely loved animal go from their lives is so difficult. It becomes even more complicated when you are friends or feel close to the people involved. Their pain becomes your pain.

Tom and Arlene D'Agostino were two such people. Though I'd not personally met them, I knew them well through the publishing process of Tom's highly successful ghost books highlighting the New England area

Tom and Arlene D'Agostino, Cooney's dad and mom, who do "the good work" all over New England. *Photo courtesy of Thomas D'Agostino.*

64

Cooneys is a cat that is determined to "do the good work" and her help with coralling animals in my Core Group was invaluable. *Photo courtesy of Thomas D'Agostino.*

(*Haunted Rhode Island, Haunted Vermont, Haunted Massachusetts,* and many others). When talking on the phone to Tom, he told me of his beloved Cooneys, a beautiful gray and white cat that had cancer. Cooneys had been a member of their family for many years and I could feel the pain Tom felt as he told me about her disease and that he expected that the final days were upon them.

One concern for most animal lovers deals with the actual process of moving from this life into the hereafter. We often worry about their last moments and whether the transition will be difficult or painful—will they even understand what is happening to them?

Anita Curtis, in her workshop, told us that everyone has spirit guides, and animals are no different. Prior to death, a spirit guide for the animal comes to them from the other side. These guides can be those known from other lives or a greeter from a "next job." That guide coaches the soon-to-pass animal, explaining the entire process. "There is no confusion or fear," says Anita. "They don't go alone." (I have come to believe that this is the same for humans.) This would be important for Cooneys, because she herself would come to be a greeter of many such souls.

One afternoon, on my way home from work, I made the immediate effort to tune into Cooneys to see how she was doing. In seconds, she was there and I was able to ask her whether she was in any pain from the cancer. She advised me that it was not pain per se, rather just that she knew that she was nearing the other side now. She preferred to be alone, under the bed, a good deal of the time because she was already starting to "do the good work" with more zeal than before. Cooneys talked about doing the "good work" a lot—a whole lot—but I'll talk more about that in a minute.

I asked about her time to pass over—was it now? She told me that no, she wanted to stay and do some good

Tom D'Agostino. *Photo courtesy of Thomas D'Agostino.*

work with Tom and Arlene for a while yet. She said that she would come to them to tell them when it was time—they would know and recognize the sign. She didn't want her human family to feel bad or sad over this. It was her plan to cross over; then she would do the good work full time for a few months or longer on the other side. After that, and if Tom and Arlene wanted, she would reincarnate or walk into another cat to do more good work with them. She wanted some time, though, after passing, to help some of the other animals on the other side. She would routinely check in with her human family and they would see the signs of her visits because they understood the good work.

I should stop for a moment to say that by this point in my ongoing training, I'd talked to many animals of varied species and I'd gotten into the habit, on the way home from work each day, of talking to animals I knew, who came to me randomly. Additionally, animals I'd talked with in the past often checked in to say hi or give me messages to pass along to someone. I was beginning to develop what I call a *core group* and this time driving home each day was what I called my Open Session. In the group, were, of course the Brooks animals, three cats, a horse, my own deceased Tessa, and my current dog, Rufus, and cat, Murphy—all who you will hear about later. Unfortunately, I spent a significant amount of my drive time organizing who would be talking next to discuss an issue. Bentley was always trying to talk over everyone else.

Cooneys was about to solve that problem for me.

Now, Cooneys is a cool cat and was not like any I'd met to that point. First, though she was lovable, she was also quite serious. She liked what I was doing (the animal communications) and had decided that she would help me "do the good work" by leading animals in for me when needed and translating if there was difficulty. She was in and out of the body already as she moved closer to the other side from her life here, and this was fun for her. She had been watching me for a few days, she told me.

She also told me that her owners, Tom and Arlene, did the good work, too, and have for years—

but she couldn't always participate. I realized then that she was talking about ghost hunting and this was a part of doing the good work, just as communication with her and other animal species.

I, of course, welcomed her with open arms (figuratively). She could help me with the animals anytime she chose, because I certainly didn't have a handle on it. So, as I moved forward in talking to the animals, Cooneys has been there regularly. She helped line up chats during any Open Session just like a little herder. She'd put them in line and kept order. And with the group I'd developed, that wasn't always easy. She had her job cut out for her.

As I write this, Cooneys is now fully on the other side—and missed a lot by Tom and Arlene—but she continues her help to *animal kind* in my core group and has been invaluable to me during my quest. I couldn't do it without her.

4. The Trouble with Walk-ins
Tessa, Latté, Rufus, and Spiderman

"Walk-Ins occur when a weakened spirit is leaving a physical body and an available and willing spirit-in-limbo acknowledges an opportunity for it to grow stronger by rejuvenating that Identity."

~www.earthtym.net

Once I'd learned how things usually worked in these animal productions of this life and the next, and the general rules for communicating with them, I began to think, without realizing it, that I truly knew how things worked. I had a multitude of knowledge to impart to anyone who listened or who needed my help. You see, I'd learned these things at seminars and from the other animal communicators I'd come in contact with since my training. I was a pro.

My heart was in the right place.

I was quick to let people who were suffering know that they could have their animals back in the form of reincarnation or through the process of walking in. I was very sure of myself, because spirit had not only spoken to me, it had taken me on a ride through the forests. I was ready to convey my knowledge.

Reincarnation, I believed, most people had an understanding of—in a human way. It is much the same for animals. If you are a believer in such things—and after some of the animal things I've seen, I certainly believe—an animal can come back in the form of another animal. The animal returning, though now a new animal in a new animal body, can be recognized by varied small little personality quirks or signs. This usually includes the death of one animal to be reanimated into babyhood (kitten, puppy, foul, etc.) body of a newly born animal.

Walk-ins—or "come-backs" as some animal communicators call them—are a bit more complicated, but I had explaining it to mourners down to a science. An animal could walk into another animal's body, take over that body with new life, as long as the animal currently residing agreed.

A situation promoting this might be where a horribly abused animal has been rescued and lay unhappy and wanting to die in a shelter. That animal might choose to forfeit life to another animal wishing to come back in a form other than a baby to start a new (and better) life. At Anita's workshop, I even met a young woman who seemed to have a cat walk-in to her current cat, but only for a visit.

This same thing seemed to be the case for my own daughter, who had lost a cat some years back. Her deceased animal, came back to visit by sharing the body of another of her cats from time to time.

Sounds simple. And I was the one to explain this to people, telling them when I'd had a communication from their animal and that this was possible for a particular situation. The cut and dry cases came very easily and I was quite pleased with how I'd handled both the animals and the calming of their humans.

But my animal guides had other ideas for me. Things were not that easy. (They never are, are they?) My training was to truly commence as I dealt with my own deceased pet, Tessa.

Mommy, I'm Coming Back— Eventually!

Back during that time in the Lancaster Park, when Donna Doyle talked with me about my own dear Tessa, she talked about *come-backs*. Telling me that Tessa's life was intimately hooked to my spirit, she explained that Tessa and I had the ability to be reunited again—in another animal. Tessa could come back as a puppy or as a *walk-in*.

Now, I understood the concept of reincarnation and do believe in it, so hearing that Tessa could come back from the other side to be my puppy

again was a very cool and welcome thing. In fact, I was trying very hard not to jump up and down.

Still, I'd read a book many years ago about *people* walk-ins, but it had not been described as a positive thing—it sounded more like possession to me. This, however, was something entirely different. Donna explained to me that if an animal in the *here-and-now* was having a horrible life, it might choose to move on to the other side and relinquish its body to a new entity—or in fact, another animal that wanted to come back to this life from the other side.

Donna told me that Tessa did indeed want to come back to me but that she'd just gotten there, on the other side, and wanted to stay a while longer.

She also told Donna that our other dog, Rufus, had some major medical problems and needed all our attention right away. This turned out to be

Rufus Roseberry was diagnosed with congenital heart disease the day after Tessa died. For a while, we though we were going to lose him, as well.

71

very true as he was diagnosed with congestive heart failure the very next day. She did not want to come back just then, but when she did decide it was time (along with me and my input), she might like to come back as a smaller dog and definitely white in color. (Remember this; it's important later.)

Donna advised that I was not to pine for Tessa or implore her to come back right away. She needed time on the other side. I was informed that when the time was right, I'd know. I'd been told this about many things in my life, and for the most part, I think that I could indeed tell when the time was right for things. Of course, there were plenty of mistakes in the timing of this kind of thing as well. But I at least understood the concept. I would wait until the time was right. Tessa would let me know—somehow. I had faith.

Once I'd talked with Donna that beautiful morning, I was able to go on with my life and put Tessa out of my mind. My grief had been relieved and I was able to again move forward. It was a blessing and one I'm truly grateful to her for, as this was not something I was able to do for myself. Seventeen years having my little Tessa weighed heavily on me—she was like a child to me.

Now, it wasn't that I was able to entirely forget her or push all the sadness away…I still was provided with the reminder every so often when I'd be in a situation where I was exposed to a prior dog behavior or item. "Unicornless" comes to mind. It was Tessa's favorite toy—a white unicorn. She'd promptly chewed off the horn on it's head, thus the strange name became associated with the toy.

After her death, it would turn up every so often in the weirdest places. I'm not saying that her ghost was moving the toy around. It could be, but the stuffed toy, long now without stuffing because I'd taken it out so she wouldn't swallow it, was also available to my other dog, Rufus. It wasn't a toy he played with, though. He didn't really play with toys very much in these later years.

Still… this little toy would stir up emotions in the pit of my stomach, as did seeing the bowl she ate from, and other varied things.

Mommy, I'm Coming Back!

So the months went on—April, May, June… My life continued as normal and I didn't think about Tessa all that much. I was just happy that she was fine on the other side. It was during this time that I began the classes with Anita Curtis. I did come into contact with Tessa during that time, but it was a learning process and not about her coming back. It was about knowing that she was truly okay and romping in fields of flowers on the other side.

Then July came. And July was weird.

One morning, I woke up and Tessa was in the forefront of my mind—not just casually, but full-blown and obsessively. She was ready to

The torn-to-pieces "Unicornless" was Tessa's favorite toy for many many years. It no longer has a horn or any stuffing, and now is just a piece of fabric shaped in the form of a horse. Spiderman took to it right away, as you can see him here with it.

come back. I knew it. I'd never been so sure of anything in my whole life. I'd spent months now with, what I'd call, healthy thoughts and grief. This was something entirely different. I was obsessed with this feeling that *now* was the time. I could be seen pacing through my home and it was difficult to stay focused on any single task. Tessa was coming back!

The trouble was, even though I was learning and had had success with communicating with animals, both on this side and the other side, I was having difficulty communicating with my own animals. Research told me that this was common and that many communicators had to see other communicators to read for their own animals. But before I did, I pulled out my pendulum for dowsing.

I'd learned the usage of this tool early on in my ghost hunting days as I wrote *Ghosts of Valley Forge and Phoenixville, Cape May Haunts,* and *Spooky York, Pennsylvania.* As an investigator for the Chester County Paranormal Research Society, my first professional exposure with the use of this tool was at a séance held at a haunted location some three years prior. Though I'd been systematically exposed to the pendulum over the

I learned about the importance of putting protections in place prior to using a pendulum as a ghost hunter. Once I had the know-how, I have found that my personal protective spirits—I call them my high-spirit committee—give the most reliable answers during my communications, though, I've interacted directly with animal spirit energy much more often than I'd talked with ghostly people during my ghost investigations.

years, this had been the first opportunity for an in-training experience with psychic and author Katherine Driver (*Philadelphia Haunts*), also a member of the group at that time. This is why I was so familiar with the concept when exposed to it at Anita's animal communications training seminar, and why I felt comfortable using it now.

The first thing I realized about using a pendulum right off was that not only does the instrument have to speak directly to its user in some ethereal connective response, but that the user's personal energy is of the utmost importance to that connection. It's interesting that spirit will specifically follow the directions set down by the person using the tool, i.e. if you tell it (rather than ask it) what a *yes* looks like and what a *no* looks like. ("Show me yes. Show me no." Or "yes swings clockwise; no swings counter clockwise.")

My idea was to try to use the pendulum to hone in on what these crazed feelings were regarding the return of Tessa. I began asking questions. Was she, indeed, ready to come back? (Yes.) Would I know her? (Yes.) Would she be a puppy? (No.) How would I find her? Through a friend? (No.) Through a shelter? (Yes.) Now we were getting somewhere. I tried then to narrow the area down where this shelter might be located.

Without going through a long process here to tell you question by question, because it takes a long time to get answers using only *yes and no* responses, I found out quite a bit of information. It came to this: Tessa was coming back to me. She could be found at the Humane League of Lancaster County, Pennsylvania, but not in the facility—rather in a foster home. She would be a light brown, very small male dog—a Chihuahua mix.

Right away I recognized a discrepancy. Donna had told me that the new Tessa would be white in color. *Hmmm.* This was not cut and dry.

75

Or, could it be that my pendulum was lying to me? Lying is a strong word, of course, but let me say that most pendulum users have found that if you don't ask exactly the right question for that exact moment, taking into consideration all affective factors, the answers you get by dowsing can be skewed. You must be so very specific when you ask questions and it may take many, many questions rather than the one in your mind to get the answers you need. Even then, with specifics listed, there may be things that could interfere—and most particulars, you won't even think about.

One big factor is that you might not know who is on the other side answering your questions. If you haven't prepared by asking to be cleared of all spirits, and that you want only to talk with your own personal guides who are both wise and caring, you might just have a spirit you don't know and who doesn't care, answering your questions. And what happens if your guides disagree? You can see how it can make the whole process a bit *iffy* at times.

Therefore, using a pendulum is not for the weak hearted. It can be maddening at times. I must say that some people have the ability to use a pendulum with letters (like those of a Ouija board), which really helps with specifics. I've not mastered that at this time. I'm still limping along with the *yes and no* regiment.

At any rate, what I'm trying to say was that my head was filled with doubts. Did this mean that Tessa had decided not to come back as a white dog, but as a brown one? And a Chihuahua mix at that. I'd never had much exposure to this breed. Still, if it was Tessa, it didn't matter if she came back as a St. Bernard (though I'd prayed that this was not the case—we could barely feed us as it was without adding a 200-pound dog to the family).

My husband, quite pragmatic, told me to stop pacing and to call the Humane League to check on it. So I kept my pendulum at the ready, asking it to swing *yes* as I was talking with the League if the animal we talked about on the phone was the right one. I called and was quite freaked out to hear the girl tell me that they did indeed have a Chihuahua mix, light brown, two years old, in a foster home. And my pendulum was swinging wide in a yes motion.

But it began to swing less dramatically as the lady told me in a later call that day that the dog in question might not be available for adoption after all—the foster family was considering adopting it.

I was devastated. Tessa would be adopted by strangers and I would remain here grieving for her. Then I remembered another part of a conversation with both Donna and Anita, the animal communicators. They'd said that the deceased animal would not come into a new body unless it was "a done deal." That is, she wouldn't come into the Chihuahua until she was in my home and the deal was sealed that the dog would be mine. I was relieved.

In my mind, I made the promise to myself that I would let this go. This dog was certainly not the one because circumstances were changing. The universe did not always react to my beck and call. I sighed, forcefully put Tessa from my mind, and moved on.

Mommy, I'm Still Coming Back!

But the plot thickens...doesn't it always?

One of the people I took my training from Anita with was Gerrie Gassert—you'll hear more about her when I introduce you to Solo, the intellectual horse—and as animal communicators go, she was hands-down a hundred times better than I was at picking things up (though she doubted herself, much as I did). We had taken to talking back and forth since we both were having trouble talking with our own animals. She had solved quite a few of my home issues with Rufus, my dog, and Murphy O'Reilley, my cat.

On this day, however, I came to her pleading. Telling her of the issues with the Chihuahua from the Humane League of Lancaster County, she became very interested and asked if I would give her a day to ponder the situation. Sometimes, and I find this to be true as well, it's easier to be alone and away from the questioner to solve a mystery—too much pressure if you are in direct contact with the human and the animal at the same time. We were, after all, beginners.

I was impatient. I wanted to know now what was going on in the world of animals and how would I reconnect with Tessa. The next day, I got an email from Gerri.

"Okay, Dinah, here's what happened this morning. My husband gets up at 4:45am and he shuts the bedroom door so our dogs stay in with me. I sit up and go through my Reiki meditation, and eventually get to the point of asking Tessa if she would like to talk to me.

"At the same moment that I feel her energy arrive, the door to my bedroom opens. Now, it had been latched, not just pulled closed. Did Tessa happen to have that ability, like my terriers do, to get just the right angle at the bottom of the door to open them? [No, she did not.]

"It freaked me out and I admit it, but after checking around the house with all the lights on, clearing the room before I entered, and starting over, she was there again.

"She told me to tell you that the messages you have been receiving are all accurate, and not to doubt. She apologized and said that this business of arranging a walk-in is more complicated than she thought. The different situations you described were all true, but she just wasn't able to make them work out. She said that she is planning to come back as soon as she can, but she is reluctant to give you any information before she is sure so that you are not disappointed again. She asks that you just relax and know that she will contact you, and to trust what you hear.

"I asked her why it didn't feel to you as though it was really her. She said that the animals remember past lives, but not when they first come back to the physical realm. The veil is there then, and gets thinner as they spend time with us. That's when we feel so close. She said to tell you that you will feel it again with her, you just have to be patient as she settles into life in the physical again.

"Her energy was very strong and she felt exuberant to me. She's anxious to make this work, and she's learning a lesson, too."

So, I of course, sat back and waited. After all, what else could I do? I certainly did not know how to make the arrangements fit my particular circumstances.

Then Gerri contacted me again. She'd heard from Tessa, unbidden. She seemed to always come to Gerri when she was practicing her meditation. Again, she told Gerri that she was planning to come back, but another idea was in the making. She'd found the perfect solution. Projecting a picture of what she would look like so that I would know how to recognize the "opportunity," Gerri described to me what she interpreted as a Yorkie, brown and black, fairly small.

I'd wrinkled my nose. A Yorkie? I'd never considered owning such a dog after meeting many

years prior a Yorkie that was so very unaffectionate that I'd turned away from the breed. It was nothing personal, but just a feeling that I'd maintained for no good reason.

Music in our home has always been important to the pets. Rufus sings a mean *Happy Birthday*, but Tessa always felt he was a show-off.

It was at this time that I'd sent Gerri a photo of Rufus and Tessa together. She immediately shot back a response that this dog, Rufus, was the dog that she'd seen—it was the colors that were important and the only reference she'd had was that of a neighbor's Yorkie. She said, "I hadn't had a chance this morning to email you to tell you to watch out for a Yorkie-colored pooch, but apparently you've already found him!"

Oh my, I thought. I knew immediately in my heart that this would be a sharing of the body and not a true walk-in. How did I know? Well, Rufus was securely happy and situated in our household and had been for nearly eight years. There would be no way that he would give up any ounce of his personality—or his food—to an "interloper." But if Tessa thought she could pull it off, this would be the best of both worlds. Both dogs in one and no new circumstances to consider. How did I know that this was too good to be true? Hmmm.

I kept my eye on Rufus intently. I wasn't seeing any change. There were no signs that Tessa was in

there with him sharing a vision of the world inside my home. Rufus was Rufus. I didn't know what to think. Then I got an email from Gerri.

"This is even weirder than usual, so bear with me. Last night I was trying to read a book but I could not concentrate; I was reading the same paragraph over and over. I realized that someone was breaking into my thoughts so I just put the book down and listened.

"It was Tessa, and she was talking in a high, squeaky, excited voice. She said she was very frustrated with this whole walk-in and sharing thing, and was very upset. Well, next thing I know, enter one of my Spirit Guides who happens to be Saint Francis.

"He asked if he could have a word with Tessa, and they went behind some sort of a barrier where I could not see or hear them. They were there for minutes of time, then he came back without her. He said she would be okay now. So I asked if I should give you a message. He said that you would already know the message, so it wasn't necessary.

"So, do you know?"

Now isn't that just like the spirit world? No, I didn't know. I hadn't a clue. And hearing that I *should* know but didn't made everything oh so much worse. But once I calmed myself—a week later, I might add—I did, indeed know. Rufus was not going to allow this sharing of a body. It was not in his nature. He never shared with her in life, to do so in death would be way out of his frame of thinking or desire. He loved his home, he loved his family, and he loved his food. He would not be taking on boarders.

Gerri reminded me, "The universe was at work here, but to what end?" That was the mystery.

So, if you're counting, two dogs down (Chihuahua and Rufus). What would happen next? I didn't think Tessa was about to give up. She wasn't the giving up kind. She was on a mission now.

Mommy, Now I'm Really Coming Back!

It Could be Fun–With Latté

The very next day at work, a close friend called me. This friend was Laurie Hull, the psychic who I'd worked many cases with. "Do you know anyone who loves dogs and might want one?" she asked me.

I perked up and then my eyes narrowed. "What kind of dog?" I asked suspiciously. A Lhasa Apso—cream colored, the color of the coffee drink. (*Hmmm.* This was near white. This

Ghost investigator and psychic medium Laurie Hull and I worked together to give Latté just the right brand of fun. Alas, synchronicity stepped in to save the day.

The sweet and energetic Latté who lives for the fun! He thought, initially, it was a good idea to share his body with Tessa.

was a small dog. And this call had come from a friend out of nowhere and on that very next day. I didn't believe in coincidences. A sign for sure.)

Latté was a two-year-old anxious dog who was giving Laurie's family difficulties since the new baby had arrived, but there were no babies in my home…both she and I felt that this would be a wonderful union. Additionally, we had a "knowing" that it was time for Latté to move on in his own spiritual search. Don't ask me how we knew this, but it was a strong psychic knowing. I wanted to meet him.

But before I went to see him, I made contact with him to discuss the issues and to get his take on what we were thinking of doing. I didn't want to make a mistake and neither did Laurie. Another surprise came to light. (Animals were full of surprises.) Latté was very interested in the situation and his personality lived for the excitement and fun side of life. He wasn't about to give up his life to let Tessa walk in as I had hoped, but suggested that she come in and share the body. It was *his* suggestion! He would be Latté and he would be Tessa—a shared coexistence. His words to me?

"It could be fun. Lots of fun. Let's have fun. Could be fun! Could be fun!"

And this, too, was something that Laurie and her family preferred—they loved him too much to see him give up his existence. Yes, a sharing was a good thing for all involved.

This would be my first real up-front-and personal exposure to the sharing of a body. And because of the way synchronicity had put Latté in front of me, I felt sure—as did Laurie—that not only was this right for me, it was right for Laurie and Latté.

I prepared my husband for the meeting by giving him specific directions. He was not to make over the dog as he was prone to do with most any animal. He was to just sit back and make no moves at all. I, too, would be of the same mind. The reason for this was because my spirit guides had indicated to me that Tessa would show me the right dog by having the animal put his paw in my lap in a waving motion. So we needed to be vigilant and watch carefully for this trick. I was determined that I would not take on any dog unless there was a sign from Tessa. We told no one about the sign—even Laurie.

Arriving at Laurie's house, we found Latté to be waiting for us in a frenzied state—he was ecstatic that we were there. And what a baby doll this dog was. But we were calm and cool. Caesar Milan would have been proud—of this part, anyway. Laurie and I chatted about ghost investigations and such and ignored the dog other than a cursory pat and scratch. Then, in the middle of our involved conversation, Latté put his two paws up on my knee and began waving one paw in the air.

"Look at him," said Laurie, "what's he doing?" She'd never seen him wave his paw like that.

That was the sign. Tessa was about to come home with us in sharing mode with Latté. I was so happy! All's well that ends well, right? Well, no, not exactly. The spirit world had other ideas about this whole little plan. And I'm finding that nothing is easy when it comes to walk-ins. It appears to be doubly difficult when there's a body sharing going on. Latté had a strong personality and lived for the fun. Though he seemed to allow Tessa in sometimes, for the most part Latté was Latté—running and jumping and causing excitement wherever he went. His mission in the world was to have fun at all costs.

The trouble was, once we got him home, he didn't really want to share that fun. He began attacking our sickly Rufus.

I was stunned. I didn't understand. Either did Laurie. He loved other dogs. What was going on? This was supposed to be the right match. Everything had lined up perfectly. Both Laurie and I went through the signs one by one. Yes, this was all

meant to be! But no. Something was missing. Aha, a lesson in synchronicity. (Oh, at times, I'm so tired of learning…) Synchronicity does not only work for one person at a time and on any clock that you might find in our own world. And it doesn't always affect just you or me. There are often threads that lead off in any number of strange directions.

So it came to pass that another acquaintance of mine who actually had a full history dealing with Lhasa Apsos was waiting for her next dog to appear. She'd been calm, but a wanting had been instilled in her that was so difficult to contain. It seemed that Laurie and I—and Latté—were part of *her* synchronicity. Life can be so complicated— you've heard the old statement, "Everything for a reason…" Okay, we get it.

So, I went down into communication mode and talked to Latté about this new development.

"Fun, fun, could be fun!" he said when the idea of moving on to yet another family was mentioned. He didn't care for Rufus very

Latté has quite the vocabulary! He told me that Rufus and him were not "simpatico!"

much, he told me. He lived for the food and not the fun. They were not "simpatico."

For Laurie and I, it hadn't been fun. Though he happily took Tessa in for a trial time, three weeks off and on, he was way over the top in the fun department and would snap or bite at anything or anyone interfering with the fun—including me. His attacks on Rufus escalated as he tried to be the head dog in the household and the instigator of fun that Rufus didn't want and, with heart disease, couldn't handle. My husband and I couldn't control him—we really didn't know how to more than anything else—and Tessa fled the union. She left us high and dry.

This was when my acquaintance made contact to tell me that she wanted him badly if I couldn't make things work. That call surprised me and made me think about all the things that had to happen for this new turn in the plan to take place.

After a discussion with Laurie, we made the decision to allow Latté to go with the person who would best make him happy at this juncture and allow him to have his fun. A happy merger. Latté moved happily on and is doing well to this day, still having fun with a whole pack of Lhasas. Both Laurie and I felt guilty for a time because we hadn't recognized the plan and were afraid that we were wrong in our interpretations and how we'd handled things, but we also had a sense that synchronicity was not something to be messed with. The world had a purpose in these things.

But there I was again. I couldn't keep taking on dogs thinking Tessa was coming back when she wasn't! It wasn't fair to me or to the dog involved. How could I depend on synchronicity every time to come to the rescue? Was I losing my mind? *Most assuredly*, I thought.

This walk-in thing that I'd so casually been telling people about was not as easy as it looked. It was fraught with problems. So, in my mind, I said,

"That's it. I'm not doing this anymore. If Tessa wants to come back, she has to make the right match, and put the right wheels in motion for me, because there is just too much heartache in it for me and everyone else."

I was learning, too, that helping others should not be quite so cavalier.

Don't Give Up, Mommy; I'm Coming Back!

The Spider Dude

Time passed. September approached and my company was having a picnic for authors from around the country that first Saturday of the month. Tessa was out of my mind. I was in picnic mode.

But not for long.

When I got home from work the Friday afternoon before the picnic, Tessa jumped into my Open Session with the animals with four feet. She was bouncing.

"I'm coming back; I'm coming back!"

Inwardly, I cringed.

"No," she said. "This time it's perfect. Black and white, just like me. Look for me, Mommy; look for me!"

No. I wasn't going to do it. I wasn't going to go down that dog path again. I went home, told my husband my thoughts, and he just laughed at me. (I don't think he really believes half of what I tell him. He just humors me.) I paced around the house, purposely staying away from my computer—which seemed to be screaming for me to come look at the PetFinder website. I don't even know where that desire came from. After about a half hour, however, I relinquished—after all, what could a little peek at the site do in the scheme of things?

I searched by zip code and then honed in on the closest rescue organization to my home: The Chester County SPCA in Pennsylvania. It took merely thirty seconds for Spiderman's picture to pop up on my screen. Black and white, small—a Japanese Chin—who looked very, very, *very* much like Tessa.

"Tessa!" I yelled out, startling my husband.

He, too, was amazed at the resemblance between this little Japanese Chin that went by the name of Spiderman and our "Pretty Little Tessa Woozle-wee" as he called her. Though smaller by about eight pounds, the Spiderman had the same coloring and the same body

When we first saw the Spiderman, we could not believe how much he looked and acted like Tessa. But this little guy had a spirit to be reckoned with that was all his own.

look. Even my husband was intrigued by this turn of events. (As a side note, when animals come back, they don't necessarily look like the animals they used to be. In fact, they could even be different animals. Tessa, however, queen that she was, had found not only the perfect dog to jump into, but one that was pleasing to her visually—that is, looked like she had these last seventeen years.) "What do you think?" my husband asked. "Are you going to call them?"

I hedged only a moment before calling the Chester County SPCA. Knowing that a full set of synchronicity events had to take place yet again before a walk-in could be established—how well I'd learned that—I asked about the history of the little guy. I was told that he'd come from a breeding kennel where he'd only been used as breeding stock. The owner had died and all the dogs had been rescued from the less than healthy and happy environment.

Hmm, I thought. This certainly was a situation where one dog might choose to allow another to take over the body. He'd been in an abusive situation and was probably tired of life in general.

But there were always kinks. I was told right away that Spiderman already had people ready to adopt him and that the facility was waiting for them to comply with regulations and paperwork the following day by 3pm—my company picnic day. I was told to call back at approximately 3:05pm that next day to see if the people had met their requirements for adoption. If not, there was a chance. I was also advised that they'd had many calls about the little fellow and that I should be prompt about calling.

I hung up with mixed emotions, but finally told myself firmly that if this was meant to be, then tomorrow the pup would be available. If not, then it wasn't Tessa, and that would be that. I would not let this make me crazy. Well, craz*ier*.

The next day held rainstorms of the torrential variety that took the picnic festivities indoors. It was, as usual, a wonderful event; but as workplace occasions would have it, I spent most of my day in small conferences—it was a work day for all accounts. At about 2pm, I was drawn into another conference, only this one had the smackings of a longer meeting. While conducting business, I watched the clock. The 3pm hour was quickly approaching and I was not in a position to leave the gathering to retreat to my office to make the necessary phone call that just might secure the Spiderman—Tessa!—in our lives. At 3:40, one meeting ended and there was talk of another. I explained my situation (these are all great people) and excused myself for a hopefully-not-too-late telephone call.

If meant to be, it would be. If not, no big deal. I kept saying it over and over in my mind.

I dialed the number and identified myself. I was put on hold. Eventually, the animal counselor came back on the line. "There's been some kind of mistake," she said. "Can you hold a bit longer?" Sure. *Well, that's that*, I thought. It wasn't meant to be.

The lady came back to the line. "Someone told you that Spiderman was not available, but he is!"

I nearly dropped the phone. She said, "But you'll need to come right now to put in paperwork, because many people have called and we're expecting a line very soon."

So, in torrents of rain, soaked to the skin, I made my way to the Chester County SPCA, making it in record time for such a miserable day. Once there, I had my first opportunity to see the little guy in person. I expected him to be jubilant to see me—after all this was going to be Tessa! He sat at the front edge of his cage, cute as anything and allowing me to stroke him through the bars, but merely glanced up at me as if to say, "Well, onto my next abusive home."

This surprised me—and broke my heart. Then suddenly I had Tessa in my head. She said, "You have to make the final arrangements before I can go in for good. I don't want to be stuck!" I looked back at the little guy, and of course, my heart melted. Yes, it was meant to be. He was a sweetheart.

I went out of the kennel and filled out the paperwork. As I was doing so, the office began to fill up—*everyone* wanted the Spiderman. What I didn't know was that this guy had been splashed all over the media—radio, television, newspapers. His sad story was everywhere and when I mentioned his name to anyone in the weeks after, I always got the same reaction, "Do you mean *the* Spiderman?!" He was a star.

But…he wasn't Tessa.

Animal Communicator Donna told me that when the shift happened—from one dog to the next—I would know it. But that it would be sometime after the dog was fully in my custody. I had high hopes. We brought our new family member home.

Those first days with the Spiderman were fraught with confusion. Was he or wasn't he? I'd not seen any shift of any kind; and Donna was away on an extended trip.

I had to laugh about some of the things going on in the house, though. Tessa had been terrified of our cat, Murphy O'Reiley, and would cower in his presence. Murphy would do all kinds of horrible things to her to keep her on edge—like jump out at her from behind furniture or swat at her from a chair as she walked under it. Tessa hated Murphy. Or if not hate, dislike was evident.

But when Spiderman arrived, his first move was to jump out from behind a chair to scare the cat! Both my husband and I felt that "turnabout was fair play." We had a great giggle at the situation. Tessa could be getting her revenge.

I began seeing more and more habits that Spiderman shared with Tessa—eating, playing, temperament in general. And little nitpicking things that made us crazy with Tessa, like the dainty way she chewed her food, thereby making giving her a pill hidden in anything nearly impossible—the Spider Dude did the same thing.

I, of course, was trying to reach Tessa through animal communications and kept getting mixed signals. Yes, she was in Spider sharing the body. No, she wasn't. Yes, she was. No, she wasn't. It was maddening.

So, not without other resources, I started calling all my psychic authors from the office to ask them to help me with the mystery. Every time, I would be told that this little Spiderman had a life all his own to be reckoned with and that Tessa was not there. So I'd call someone else—hoping that this prior reading was wrong. I just wanted ONE psychic to tell me that she was in there. But no. All felt that she was not. All of them.

Well, then I was angry. It wasn't that I didn't already love little Spiderman. I did, and nothing would make me give him up. He was a Roseberry now! But daggone, I wanted Tessa to come back, too! Now I knew how the girl in my training class felt when I'd told her that her cat was popping in and out to visit. She'd gotten several cats, thinking her one true heart animal cat was in each one, only to find that she needed to get yet one more. Cats were everywhere! I wasn't going to get another dog, but I did want to know what was going on.

Maybe this animal communication thing was not for me—I certainly wasn't getting things right. I decided again to let the whole Tessa ordeal go. I went to my spirit guides and told them (yet again) that I couldn't deal

Tessa was always bullied by Murphy O'Reilley (our cat) and was jumpy whenever he was around. But Spiderman would have none of the bullying. In fact, he loves chasing the cat and apparently feels like Murphy is his very own.

with the stress of the process. If I was supposed to know what was going on and if Tessa was indeed back or coming back, I needed some kind of proof. Then I went about my daily life.

Hope from Hope

A short time later, I was asked to attend a Mind/Body/Spirit convention in Allentown, Pennsylvania. I was excited—I loved conventions and especially those dealing with spirit, for obvious reasons. As I walked around the spirit-filled halls, looking at all the lovely services and wares to be had, I passed by several animal communicators. I had the itch. I wanted to talk to one, or all, of them. I had to know what they saw. It was like a drug addiction—I needed a fix. Where was Tessa? Who was Spiderman? I truly wanted someone to tell me that Spider was Tessa. Then I would feel guilty because I loved Spider as Spider, too.

Alas, talking to five or six different communicators can get quite expensive, so I strolled around and around waiting to feel a connection to one of them.

I knew I had that knack to decide which one was for me. I just had to focus. Who would be the best communicator for me this fine day?

I finally settled on Hope Pollock, an animal communicator and Reiki Master for Critter Chatter in Wyomissing, Pennsylvania. I walked up to her table and sat down in the chair provided. My first thought was not to tell her that I, too, was a communicator, but quickly decided to be truthful, knowing that in reversed situations, I'd want to know. She became very animated when she found out that we shared this skill and I soon found out that she, too, had been a student of Anita Curtis.

I told her very little about Tessa, though. I needed to know if Tessa would talk with her before I opened up with my long dilemma. There were so many around me these days. It didn't take long for me to know that she had the gift. She described Tessa to the "T" and told me how strongly she was coming in—a bouncing personality full of life and love. Each time I'd talked with someone, I had been told this same thing.

Then the mystery started to unravel. Hope told me that she felt a very unsettled emotion coming from Tessa. She wanted to come back desperately to be with me. ...But, she just wasn't entirely sure. She was so very happy on the other side, though she missed me a lot. Her mind was not made up despite the signals she'd been sending out to the universe to me. And now there was a further issue. She'd waited so long to make her decision, that the Spiderman was not as keen on opting out for her as he had been while sitting in the lonely kennel at the SPCA.

Spiderman was coming into his own and having a blast at our house. Not only did he get continual love and full run of the house, he loved our other dog, Rufus, and felt like he had his very own cat. He ate great food, took walks, and could be out on the fenced deck looking at cars and people. He had toys. He had two beds.

If Spider wasn't Tessa, he was missing a really good chance.

Spiderman is very serious about his snacks since he came from a place where such a thing was not part of his life. If he does not have the desire to eat it right when given, he guards the snack by carrying it around in his mouth all day—or at least until he's hungry again. (It took no time at all to find out that Rufus sniffs out hidden snacks—no matter who they belong to and Spider was taking no chances.)

He could get on the furniture and eat some people food. Spider was having second thoughts about the whole giving up the dog situation.

But having promised Tessa to be part of the arrangement, he was willing to stand by his agreement, though saddened by it. Still, Tessa was uncertain.

I asked Hope what would happen if she walked into Spiderman and changed her mind again like what had happened with Latté. Would Spider be back? Hope said no. If Tessa took over entirely and then departed Spiderman's body, there would be no soul in Spiderman and he would die.

Well, that piece of advice got my heart ticking. This situation was much worse than I'd thought. I made a decision right then. "Hope," I said. "I don't want Tessa to feel any remorse about staying on the other side. I will be fine without her—I can communicate with her anytime. She needs to be where she is happy. Indecision means that she is not ready to commit and I think she should stay on the other side. And Spiderman should remain here with me. He deserves to have his life."

Hope relayed the message and then told me that she felt like a heavy blanket had been lifted from her. Tessa's main reason for coming back was for me, and knowing that I did not need her to make that gesture, and that I would still love her even on the other side, gave her great comfort.

So the Spiderman was here to stay. And he told Hope that he was very happy about the turn of events.

So. All's well that ends well, as I said before. Except…

Tessa went off to the fields of flowers on the other side, and Spiderman took his rightful spot in the Roseberry house and in our hearts. But there was still turmoil that had me baffled and very bothered. Spiderman had taken on so many personality traits that were specific to Tessa that I was continually questioning whether or not she'd really stayed on the other side or whether she was popping in and out. Every time I turned around, Spider was exhibiting a

behavior pattern that was not like his own, but was very much like Tessa. My husband had even begun calling him the "Woozle," which was his pet name for Tessa. And I've been known to say time and again, "If Spider isn't Tessa, he's missing a damn good chance."

So I put it out of my mind, again. The decision had been made anyway. Tessa would be on the other side. These things that the Spider Dude did were coincidences. …Wait, I don't believe in coincidences. *Hmmm.* Do you see the problem?

Time moved forward.

Mommy! No, Not Again!

It wasn't too long before author and sensitive Lee Prosser, of *Missouri Hauntings* fame, began sending me emails asking whether I'd had contact with my little dog who had passed away. This was unlike him. Though he kept regular contact with me because I have been one of his editors over the prior year, to have this sensitive contact me routinely asking about my dog was a bit mysterious to me.

Each time he asked, I would say: "No, have *you* heard something from her?" His answer was always that there had been some kind of connected feeling around the dog and me that he'd been aware of, but he couldn't put his finger on the nature of the feeling. He was certain it was a positive thing, and under other circumstances, he would dismiss such a tweak to his inner guidance. Still, he knew that

I'd been so sad about the death of Tessa, and felt he needed to contact me about her.

One day, not only did I get an e-mail from him asking the same question, but a telephone call soon followed. He asked yet again.

I thought about it a few seconds. Although it was true that I had seen her in my Open Sessions quite frequently, and she did show a bit of excitement that hadn't been there of late, I still did not have an idea of what kind of sensitive feelings he was having about her. He seemed to have the sensation that she was about to make some kind of big decision. He was questioning me to find out whether I was still grieving so badly that I was holding her here close to Earth or whether there was some other kind of decision afoot.

I thought about that, too. I truthfully felt that over the past months, and since there had been

Author and sensitive Lee Prosser helped me navigate the spiritual nightmare that Tessa was dragging me through day by day. Here he shows us the animals that "own" him—Frank and Barry, the very lovable Siamese cats. *Photo courtesy of Lee Prosser.*

varied things requiring a great amount of attention sucking up the fabric of my sensitivities, that I had gotten through the grieving process. In fact, I rather welcomed her ghostly input in my open sessions and found that to be enough to easily sustain me.

But here Lee was, questioning me. I thought a little bit more about the situation and delved deep into my own heart to see if I, indeed, was still holding her captive here with me. Shaking my head, I still felt as though this were not the case.

On the way home from work that day, I had my usual Open Session with the animals. Tessa was there again and this time she was incredibly bouncy—even more so than usual. And things that were coming to my mind from her were scary. There was even a short moment when I felt that I needed to hold up a mental cross in my mind to keep away what she was about to tell me—because I knew what was coming.

"I'm coming back!" she said in my mind (again).

I freaked out. Now, it wasn't that I didn't want her to come back. I loved her dearly and would always love her. But I'd been through all this before (four times now) and it was quite harrowing to think that I could survive it yet another time.

Not only that, but because of these back and forth coming-back scenarios, we'd invited the new Spiderman into our household. So now, not only did my husband and I live in our home, but Rufus, a very sickly dog with congestive heart failure, the new little twelve-pound Spiderman whose delicate stature was sometimes cause for health concern, and a big bushy hungry Murphy O'Reilley the cat. There was just no room for another addition. I even questioned in my mind the ability to afford the upkeep of another pet, considering the downturn of the economy. I was worried whether I was able to manage a livelihood for ourselves without thinking of another mouth to feed and care for.

I knew of one thing that was an absolute: If ever I invited Tessa back from the other side, it would be at a time when I could provide her a wonderful life with everything she needed. I didn't want to scrimp and save and worry whether she got the appropriate veterinary care or whether she had the right foods to eat. Her life needed to be perfect; otherwise why come back from the other side where she was so happy already?

My final thought brought back all the anguish I had gone through trying to understand whether or not she was indeed even coming back the first time, whether I was getting the right impressions from my own mind and other animal communicators, and wondering whether she was still around. In my mind, I threw up my hands and I said, "Okay Tessa, here's the story. You are, of course, welcome to come back. I would love to have you back. But *this* time, *I'm* not sure. It has to come from the top down: God, the Angels, spirit guides, and you have to work it out altogether before you involve me. I don't want to go to shelters. I don't want do any legwork. I don't want to know anything about anything. Basically, you need to show up on my porch for me to even get involved in this. I want to know for certain that all parties involved want and need this to happen. There should be no thinking required on my part. I want to be able to be prosperous enough to take care of you; I want our home to be a welcome place for you; I don't want there to be any confrontational issues between you and the other animals within our household. I want it to be a perfect situation that is planned and blessed from the top down. Or...I don't want it. And I mean it this time."

Oddly—because there is no perfect situation that I know of—I got a consensual nod from my spirit guides, and even Tessa was happy with what I'd said (which was a scary thing). When I reached my home, my husband greeted me with a newspaper. On the front page of that paper he pointed out a picture of a black-and-white dog. I just looked up at him as he said, "You have to read this. Apparently, there is a group who is giving away a great deal of money to shelters across the country to increase the number of animals adopted. Each shelter involved is going to give away adoptions of ten free animals, first come-first serve, with all fees taken care of."

I looked at him and said, "Why are you telling me this?" He shrugged.

I walked away thinking, *Oh my God*! What are the odds that he would show me something like this after my interactions with Tessa at the Open Session? I was a softy for any sheltered animal. As he went into the living room away from me, I looked up to the ceiling and said, "Not good enough; I do not want to go to the shelter. And I need more money than just a waving of fees."

I repeated in my mind to my animal spirit guides that if Tessa's was to come back to me, yes, it would be cool if she looked like the old Tessa in some fashion so that I would know her. And yes, I guessed that I didn't want fees involved either; but there were a lot of other things I'd mentioned that had to take place. First and foremost, one of those things was that the animal needed to come directly to me. I would not search it out, nor did I want to conduct the research involved in finding yet another new pet. And I wanted to be able to afford it—which was not the present case. In fact, I didn't even WANT a new pet. It had to be a Godsend.

Again there was a consensual nod. But it had me on edge. What would happen next? Were the powers-that-be getting me used to the idea?

In the meantime, as I've stopped thinking about it, Spiderman often stands on my end table looking at me at the computer—something Tessa did all the time, despite my yelling at her to get down, because this was not allowed—and he plays the trickster with his food, another Tessa trait. Both these things got on my last nerve then, and now.

What's going on?!

Having a Ball

Of course, trying not to think about something is a difficult thing to do—especially when there are tiny little reminders and nudges that keep pawing at the brain. Author, sensitive, and friend, Lee Prosser, was one of these nudges, not that he was doing harm, but boy could he guess my state of mind. And Tessa's.

It was in January of 2009 that he called me to tell me that he'd had a vision of Tessa. (*Oh no!* I thought. *She's still at it!*) He told me that he saw her in the field of flowers, very happy and playing with an orange or red ball the size of a tennis ball. I frowned. The field of flowers was on the first floor of my meditation place in my elevator scenerio—the place of comfort and religious significance for me. But Tessa never played with balls—ever. In the seventeen years she'd been with me, not once had I ever been able to urge her to chase a ball. Oh, she'd rip the hell out of a stuffed toy and eat the insides out of it if she could, but no ball.

Lee seemed to feel that this ball had significance, however. He'd also been a tad confused because Tessa also told him that he should write a book about time travel. So what was this about? Did she really want him to write such a book, and why was she looking for authors as I did in my day job? Or was she telling me that I had to learn to—please don't laugh at me here—navigate the world beyond through time travel or some other time manipulation? Was Lee visualizing messages for me or for himself? As usual, I was stumped.

A day or so later, Lee emailed me to tell me that he'd seen her again—she was nothing if not persistent. This time, she had the ball and was wearing a pointed hat with a velveteen purple witch star symbol on one side and the word "Om" (as seen in meditation) on the other. Bizarre? Yes. But there's more. At the start of the pathway, which was not far from the place where the dog was playing with the ball, was a large letter, "L." He didn't know if it was a signpost between worlds or dimensions or had some other meaning. It was large and painted in a satin white color that reflected the sunshine about the area.

I didn't have a clue regarding what the hat, symbols, letter, and signpost meant except maybe that I'd used these spiritual methods to stay in touch with her by trial and error paths. (Anyone reading this with an idea of what it means, I'm all ears.) My only witch involvement these days was with Marla Brooks (Bentley's mom) and her witchcraft book... more mysteries.

So I attempted to go into my animal communications state to ask about the vision. The answer from my guides was simple and matter-of-fact. I was told to keep my eyes open for the red ball.

Okay. Clear as mud. So now you'll find me looking for red balls.

Wait, I thought! *PowerBall! That's certainly red!* That would definitely provide me with the means to take on another dog in the family (if I didn't consider the fact that spirit does not reward in lottery). Let's all keep our fingers crossed anyway.

...Because I don't really know anymore now then I did then.

In my next chapter, you will be meeting Mary Gasparo more intimately, but for now, this good friend who works ghost cases with me had an empathic vision about Tessa in March of 2009. As you can see, Tessa always leaves me alone for a couple months before she comes up with the next item on the agenda.

Mary told me that she had the feeling that Spiderman was a litter mate, or from another litter from the same parents in a different life as Tessa. This was why I'd been drawn to the shelter pup. She also thought that Tessa was now going to wait

Tessa talked with Anita Curtis to tell her that everything had changed regarding her walk-in status.

for Rufus to join her on the other side before making any decisions about coming back. After all, she was the big sister and she wanted him to see how things were. Mary thought that the newspaper *nudge* was a test (I hate tests) and that I'd passed it. Tessa, for the time being, was hanging back.

But Mommy, I Said I Was Coming Back!

As I was putting my Tessa story together, I had occasion to contact Anita Curtis who, for me, is responsible for bringing to light this wonderful ability and to whom I will be forever grateful. She'd offered to write my Foreword and I was ecstatic to hear it! On the day I spoke with her, she said to me right away, "Things have dramatically changed in your situation with Tessa."

Okay, I thought, *change is good. Sometimes.* But I was wary. It didn't take a rocket scientist to know that she was about to upset my apple—I mean animal—cart. Tessa was at it again.

Anita had been in touch with the bouncy Tessa, who already knew I would be talking with her in this short span before the completion of my book and her story.

Anita first told me that all that had gone on before with Tessa was true and correct. I'd read the right signs and talked to the right people. But all that aside, the universe had different ideas about my just, well, giving up, on my sweet dog relation coming back into my life at this point. Yes, things had changed.

Anita let me know that Tessa had been very frustrated with the whole situation and this, of course, was something I'd surmised from one bad incident after another. Yes, my little dog was sorry about the things that had gone wrong, but the last

try, with Spiderman, had been well planned out. She had "sent" Spider to me. Things had been worked out down to every detail. Every piece had fallen into line according to Tessa's arrangements.

But Anita told me that it was Tessa's angry belief that Spiderman broke the contract that had kept the wheels of change in motion, even though I'd decided not to pursue. Spider had refused to allow Tessa to take over completely. He'd broken his promise to her.

Oddly (or not), my feelings that Spider had decided that life in the Roseberry house was a fantastic change from his prior existence were right on. There was also, though, confusion. Once with us and happy, he was confused about what waited for him on the other side. And there was fear. He'd found his Heaven, in effect, with us and was very reluctant to move on now that he'd become situated in our lives. As Anita says, "He couldn't imagine anything better than what he had now." The little dog *had* to break the contract because what awaited him would surely be horrendous in comparison.

So, during this breather that spirit had given me, Tessa sat back and allowed the guides and God to explain the way it was on the otherside to the fearful Spiderman. We, of course, are not entirely in that circle of understanding, but Spider was, in some fashion, given a grand tour.

When Anita contacted me, Spider knew things he'd not known before. He was meant to make the agreement with Tessa—she'd saved him from the pound. He'd discovered that he was to be happily situated on the otherside—learning and healing and growing in spirit. He would continue, and he would be confident and joyful as he did it.

Spiderman was okay with the switch now. The original contract again was in place. Anita advised me that exciting Thursday afternoon when I spoke with her, that Tessa was planning on taking over Spider's body in thirty hours. The deal was signed and sealed.

Thirty hours! That would be Friday evening at 8:30pm. In roughly a day and a half, little Tessa would be back in my life. "I shall return!" she'd said to Anita in a happy tone, one that reflected a light nature and lovely sense of humor. She'd told Anita that the best body to come back in had already been taken though—her old one! Spiderman's would have to do.

I went home that day from work bouncing just like my little Tessa.

The Weird Watch

At 8:15pm Friday night, Spiderman sat on his blanket with all his toys under the coffee table. He looked just like Spiderman, sitting there in a Sphinx pose looking out at his living room domain.

My husband remarked, "This is weird watching the dog like this. I think she's already in there." He'd seen, as I had, how since Anita's call, the personality quirks that Tessa had displayed throughout her life had taken over the normalcy of Spider's persona. I had to admit, it was, indeed, strange. I, too, could swear that the swap had been completed.

But Anita had impressed upon me that until the change was formally made, this reflection of

Although Spiderman looks a lot like Tessa, it was difficult to really put our minds around one dog walking into another.

character that we were seeing (and had seen over the prior months) indicating that she was there, and then not, was only her influence on Spider. She was pushing her thoughts and actions on the little guy. Anita advised that the final shift would be very subtle once it occurred.

Let it be noted here that Rufus had been throwing up all day in a sort of stressful waiting pattern. He paced. He snubbed his food—this never happened. And he threw up more. This dog knew a powerful change was coming. I'd tried to communicate to him earlier what the circumstances were and Anita had alerted him on the prior day. Still, Rufus hated change. If we moved a chair in the house to a new location, it upset him for days. Now he was lying out of the way on the rug, watching us watch Spiderman.

At 8:30, we sat staring at the dog. He sat staring at us.

"I don't see anything," said my husband.

"Me neither," I replied.

So after about a half hour, we stopped watching and things went back to what we'd thought to be normal.

"I still say she's already in there," said my husband when we went to bed.

The next morning at breakfast was my first indication that Spider was gone and Tessa was indeed back and in charge as she'd always been. Spider had been very happy with his food. He ate dog food. A little wet mixed with the dry for flavor. He was a good eater and not at all picky—except when I felt he was being influenced by Tessa as in the bowl he ate from. He would only eat from her old bowl—which was a seventeen-year-old hard-style Tupperware—not his nice new shiny one that we'd purchased just for him. Today, he would not eat. He looked at the food and then up at me as if to say, "You've got to be kidding." Then he turned and left the area.

"No," I said out loud. I would not succumb to the idea that people food had to be mixed in Spider's food in place of the wet dog food. This was a maddening Tessa trait. She would literally starve herself for days just to get a piece of hotdog mixed in her food. And

I'm ashamed to say that she usually won out. She was spoiled rotten. This was Tessa alright.

"She's back," I told my husband when he came into the room.

"Yup, I know," he said. "Spider's peeing on his blanket to keep Rufus away. He's the woozle for sure."

So Tessa was back, and she'd brought back all the bad habits that Spider didn't have. Oh well, all's well that ends well. (Where have we heard that before?) Or is the saying, "Be careful what you wish for?"

Guilty Pleasures

The bad habits were not really that big a deal. It was Tessa, and we loved her. Further, she had so many other good habits. And wonderfully enough, since this dog body was a new one for her, there were traits specific to the breed that were equally loving. Some of Spiderman's habits were retained there as well. Tessa was now the Spiderman.

I must say though, that the guilt returned pretty quickly. *Why?* you might ask. After all, this was what we'd wanted all along!

Yes, that's true...but we really did love Spiderman as well. The first Spiderman, that is. He was a little joy and sending him to the otherside felt much like sending him to his death. My own guides have implored that I not feel this way and Anita, too, lovingly told me that he was so happy now and that he'd been given a blessing. In my head, I knew this was true. But it was a hard pill to swallow for my heart and one I've been struggling with since the switch.

But Tessa, I mean Spiderman (cuz he no longer uses the Tessa body and gender), is giving me time. She has settled into the new body and now is in the state of forgetting—which happens when one returns from the otherside. Now she is just our family member, happy and content—but with a will to be reckoned with.

I've invited the first Spiderman to belong to my Core Group and he's considering the invitation—there's much for him to do right now. And I find it

Anyone who loves animals will understand the guilt we felt at the thought of little Spiderman going off to the otherside—regardless of the contract made between Tessa and him.

confusing to see him in the same persona as the dog living in my home. Equally confusing is that Tessa reveals herself as her first body when she comes to the core group.

I'm getting used to it and the guilt is diminishing with each day. But it's not entirely gone, and unfortunately, I really don't think it will ever go entirely away. I miss the first Spiderman. It's that old adage of eating cake. "You can't have your cake and eat it, too." Or if you can, the icing might not be chocolate. One has to deal.

Lessons Learned

One thing I was sure of through all this walk-in process, was that I was going through it to learn exactly what the ropes were. It was all part of spirit's plan. This was important if I were to be advising other folks that this could happen for them. It wasn't always as easy as I'd assumed and things didn't always make sense or go as planned.

There was actually a mental slap at how easily I spilled forth words of comfort to people, promising them that there was the probability that their animal could come back as a walk-in or reincarnated baby animal. There were multiple sides and issues here to be considered—and there were no guarantees or guidelines. I had no right to mention such a promise without advising the person that this was not a perfect science. I became aware that I did not hold the reins—and unfortunately, but without knowing it, I'd felt I had been holding them. The truth was, in most cases, not only didn't I hold the reins, I didn't even have a horse.

I'd had further time to think about and talk to my guides about Lee's vision of the "L" sign on the path and the witch hat with "Om" on the side. I felt that the "L" stood for my animal guides the leopard and lemur pointing me via road sign located at the forest in my visualization to meditate as per the suggestions of friend and witch, Marla Brooks (thus the witch hat). I'd also heard the same advice from Beckah Boyd of Ghost Quest fame. I'm still looking for the red ball, though. And still hoping for the lottery.

Tessa's take on all this via Anita Curtis? And by the way, she was specific that everyone in the world know that the following was *her* quote and her gift to the world. She wanted to be personally credited only as: Tessa. While her quote didn't seem, at the time, to personally advise me, she showed me that the spiritual side of life was to be aware of and to look at the big picture. There was something larger at stake than just living in love within a family. Her message was for compassion and love for the masses. She said through Anita:

> "We must all learn to practice forgiveness to live peacefully together."
>
> ~Tessa

I'm afraid the lessons are not over yet—for any of us.

Tessa's message had meaning for all man and animal kind: "We must all learn to practice forgiveness to live peacefully together." If an animal recognizes the validity of this statement, why can't we all see and practice it?

5. Mary Had a Little Cat....or a Bunch of 'em
Gracie, Lilly, Belle, BJ, Shadow

"I am a firm believer, that everything happens for a reason. Fate definitely puts into play what life holds for us. Do we have the free will? Yes, but I think our guides do have a little input as to which way we take the path. Once in awhile, we are allowed to make mistakes, but then we learn and hope the choices we make are always for the best."

~Mary Gasparo

Mary Gasparo is a woman wearing many hats. In her day job, she works in kitchen design and has an eye for what looks right in the world, and in between the minutes and hours of her days, she is a breeder of Persian and Himalayan kittens, saves cats and kittens, and runs a rescue organization that is no less than miraculous at helping those who cannot help themselves.

Then, at night, well, it's an entirely different story. In fact, she's just as bizarre and kooky as I am—she's a ghost hunter, too. And as is with most ghost hunters, there were always mysteries to be solved.

Mary Gasparo, a woman with more than one hat— and more than one cat! *Photo courtesy of Laurie Hull.*

Mary, though, had more than mysteries to solve. Her issues were all mixed up with day-to-day cat issues as well as a pesky ghost. So she was happy to hear that I was taking on clients in an effort to practice, practice, practice this skill of animal communications. Did *she* have an animal (or ten) for me! Where had I heard this sentiment before?

The interesting thing—or scary, depending on your frame of mind—is how much of what I'm about to tell you is connected. Occurrences seem to happen independently of each other in the animal world (as in our own world, it would seem), but when one really looks close and tries to unravel the knotted threads of lives, it's pretty darn clear that an interconnection of grand proportions is at play.

The way the world confuses the issue (and us) has much to do with chronological order—or the lack of it. Sometimes, one will find that an incident that occurs much later in a scenario, is a prominent part of what happens in the beginning of another situation. Don't even try to figure that out. The same holds true that an incident occurring a year

earlier, may very well affect what happens today or tomorrow—almost in preparation of a new coming event. Still other things are happening simultaneously and seemingly independent of each other. Have I totally confused you? Well then, my job here is almost done, for the following interactions with Mary and her wonderful cats jumps around through the weeks, months, years, and days all culminating in one place and one time—now.

So. Let us delve into the next mysterious world of cats.

By the Grace of God

I will begin by describing Mary's cat, Gracie, since she was the first of Mary's "babies" that I communicated with during my beginning trek. When I first "met" Gracie, she was one sick little kitty and I had no concept that at one time she was a vital presence in the Gasparo household. In fact, she was in the hospital and probably near death when I came into the picture.

Gracie, part of my Core Group of animals, was part of a great mystery to be solved. *Photo courtesy of Mary Gasparo.*

Stepping back to her past, six years prior, however, she was not always in such dire straits. Mary told me her history.

"My original cat, BJ, who was ten years old at the time, was starting to show her age. My husband and I thought it best to get another cat. You see, BJ was, and is, such a good cat,

we thought a new one could learn from her. My son, at the time, worked at a local pet shop. Each week we would go and look at all the kittens, but none called out to me. One of his coworkers had a Persian kitten for sale (he was a breeder outside of work). So, we took a look at her and still…nothing. I have always been a domestic short-hair cat lover. I, also, was one who followed the cat plight rescue. So to pick out a pure breed that was not rescued from the local shelter, was unheard of for me.

"Two days after the first meeting of the six-week-old Persian cutie, I was telling a friend about her and how she reminded me of her grand daughter. Just then, I felt a twinge and I knew that the little kitten was going to be mine.

"Six years have passed and the little kitten is now known as Gracie. She is the most beautiful Persian (at least in my eyes) you would ever see. Gracie has blessed me, and others, with her babies. I bred her only

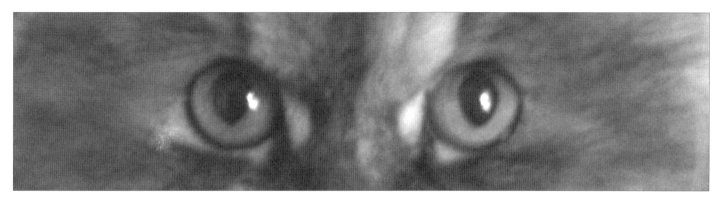

twice, because her body is not designed to be a breeding cat. I kept two of her daughters…. Daisy and Dori. Life around our home has never been the same since I let that little kitten into my heart!"

Of course, this all happened prior to my meeting Mary and Gracie in real life, and I had no idea that when Mary joined the paranormal group I belonged to— CCPRS, Chester County Paranormal Research Society (yes, a mouthful) that we would become such quick friends. It was pretty much instantaneous and we both felt that we'd known each other our whole lives. This, by the way, could have been a clue that fate was in play—or if not fate, some paranormal connection that was long ago played out to bring us to a certain place and time. For those believing in reincarnation— most all animal communicators I've talked to know this to be a fact—the feeling of "knowing someone before" is an indication that indeed, there was a relationship in a prior life.

Here the plot thickens, but no one suspected just how thick it was and how many lives would be affected adversely. CCPRS had taken on a very dark case. It was a mystery case where those involved could not figure out what was going on in a home we'd been called forth to investigate. This case was so dark in nature, that it was decided that only a few people within the group would become involved. It was dangerous.

I must tell you that I was one of the first persons to raise my hand to volunteer regarding this most frightening case. "Leave me out of it!" I'd said. (You didn't think I'd volunteer did you? I'm basically a chicken at heart when it comes to real danger.) "I don't want to bring home any demons, negative spirits, or bad karma. I have enough of that on my plate already, thank you very much." (Besides, my husband would have killed me.)

Thus, I was not involved and was not privy to data relating to the case. In fact, the case was "off the books" and limited exposure for all members was suggested. Still, we were all warned to keep an eye on our daily routines in life to make sure that negative occurrences were not directly related to this case—whether we were involved or not. See why I didn't want to be involved?

I don't really know anything about the situation except that there were negative energies preying on the innocent, an aggressive ghost, a person held hostage, and obsessive behaviors. I was on the outside looking in, and what I was seeing was not good—so I didn't look. Strange things began happening to some of the members of the group who were working the case. Cringing things. Things that make you know that you made the right decision to step back. Even if it was just imagination—you always had treat it like fact for your own safety.

But we're here to talk about animals. And yes, these cringing things are connected. But you'll have to wait until the end to fully grasp the hook that the world beyond has on us here right now—or yesterday, or tomorrow. It was well into the dark case that Mary noticed that Gracie was looking sick and gradually going down hill. She did not connect it to the case. This was life. Her baby was sick and a trip to the vet was in order. Gracie had gone, almost overnight, from vital and happy kitty to skin-and-bones death watch for no visible reason.

Gracie was then diagnosed with kidney failure and had little time to live if her current state continued. This was a surprise. She was hospitalized for a week and then sent home to be more comfortable—there was nothing more that could be done. Gracie was dying.

That night, Mary—a wreck and in tears—held little Gracie in her arms. She looked up in prayer and then asked her deceased father (who'd passed in 1984 an avid animal lover) if there was anything he could do to help Gracie get better. That night, Gracie nibbled at her food a bit and the next morning she ate a bit more. She didn't really think at the time that her father had anything to do with Gracie feeling just a little bit better. But when she smelled the Captain Black pipe tobacco with its distinctive smell, she knew. Her father had smoked a pipe for years and used this very tobacco making the room now fragrant. But she told no one. After all, Gracie was still dying, and who would believe that she'd felt her father?

Only those within her ghost group.

This was when Mary contacted me. It was her hope to communicate to her cat and to let her know that she loved her and would do whatever needed to be done to help her.

I was afraid. This was really the first time I'd been asked to talk with an animal who was terminally ill. This was the first time that a person in terrible pain was asking me to help with relief. This was the first time that what I said could mean wonderful or horrible things to all those involved. What if I made a mistake? What if what I was seeing was really something my mind just made up to suit the circumstances? (Here I went again—it never stops, that doubt.) But what could I do? A friend was in need. And it *just might* be true that I could communicate with the animals. Bentley was always right there during the doubt times to remind me what a pain in the butt I was. Sweet Bentley.

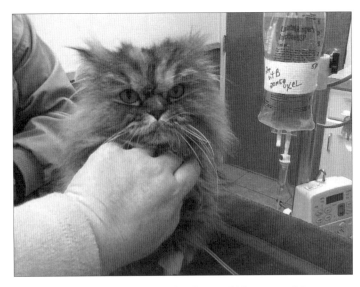

Gracie, at one point, was near death. Her kidneys would not function and she was hospitialized. We all felt the knocking of the Grim Reaper for this sweet little cat. *Photo courtesy of Mary Gasparo.*

So I agreed to read for Gracie. But I didn't do it over the telephone. I just took the photo that Mary supplied me (heartbreaking with tubes going into the wasting Grace) and sat alone to go down into my meditation. This time, I talked at length with my guides first, letting them know that this was a life and death situation and that their help would be so important. I couldn't do it alone. They just nodded and nodded, already knowing the situation and completely understanding what needed to be done.

The first thought that popped into my mind was "Pop." I felt like Pop was coming through and had visited the Gasparo household. There was a very specific order from Pop that was to go directly to Gracie. "Gracie, you must eat or you will die." I communicated this to Gracie, who listened intently, though she seemed very weak and tired. At the time, it seemed so trivial to me that this was the only thing I could get. In fact, I was mortified. How was just eating going to save the sweet little Gracie? But it was not mine to ask. What I got from the communication, was what I got. It *was*, what it was. And it didn't come from the animal, so I haven't a clue where the impression developed unless from my guides directly.

Then Gracie murmured in a soft voice (that was her voice but also mine—yeah, I know, sounds crazy…) that she loved her Mommy and could I tell her that? She also wanted Mary to know that, being so sick, she needed to get some rest and that she would need time to get better. She said that she understood her Pop, that she had to eat. And she also said that Pop had told her to tell her Mommy to lighten up!

So, not happy with what I'd gotten, but unable to get more, I took a breath and emailed Mary to tell her what I'd been told, apologizing for not having more to tell her. Later she wrote to me:

> "When I read that e-mail, I cried for quite some time. I knew in my heart that my dad had come to visit and it overwhelmed me to have you confirm it."

And oddly enough—weirdly enough—Gracie began eating and she began to get better.

However, you don't just "get over" kidney disease.

A Shadow Arrives and Leaves All Too Quickly

This is one of those places where there is a story within a story, and those odd connections build up that seem to materialize out of nowhere. My introduction to Shadow didn't really happen until much later, but I think a short description here is warranted.

Mary had a lovely neighbor, Ann, who had a cat by the name of Shadow. Shadow was named so because this trooper of a feline was a "shadow" to Ann, following her everywhere.

Now Shadow had a story to beat all stories and I'm afraid that much of it is buried beneath still another shadow, one of despair, yet with a glimmer of love attached. Shadow had been a feral cat that Ann rescued—an itty bitty thing with lots and lots of health issues. This small skittish and scrawny cat stumbled up to Ann's front door two years prior. It took a while, but she eventually began to trust and love Ann.

It was odd, but every so often Shadow would disappear for a time. In May, as this story unfolds, Shadow went missing for a couple weeks. When she finally came back, she was skin and bones, and obviously not doing well. Though Ann thought that she had been locked by accident in someone's shed, I felt that this feline child of God was out helping another unfortunate cat in the world. I kept this to myself as I listened to the story—my thoughts sounded crazy.

Ann stood beside little Shadow, and one by one, through the years had pulled the cat through each of her medical issues and lived through her little disappearances. Unfortunately, medical problems and the life of a feral animal had taken its toll on this small cat.

So it came to be that Ann had to have knee surgery and then was forced to stay at a rehabilitation facility for a few weeks. It was during this time, when a major event would occur affecting all those around Shadow. She became deathly ill and the veterinarians did all they could, but alas, Shadow's organs were shutting down and she was near death.

Ann's daughter arrived that final morning, as her mother was still at rehab, to find Shadow in a very bad way. Off to the hospital; but it was no use. Shadow's organs were failing one by one. Death was imminent. The decision was made to have Shadow put down to ease her suffering.

This happened **Tuesday, June 24th, 2008, at 4pm**.

Gracie's Shadow

In the meantime, Gracie, though feeling much better from eating as her Pop had instructed, needed a blood test for the medical professionals to determine what was happening with her failing kidneys.

This test was performed on **Tuesday, June 24th, 2008 at 4pm.**

The next day, Wednesday, June 25th, Mary's vet called to tell her that Gracie's lab work had returned showing the results of her kidney function. Mary was prepared for the worst. But the results showed that Gracie now had the kidneys of a kitten!

Thursday June 26th, an autopsy was conducted on Shadow. The vets told Ann that the only 100-percent-functioning organ Shadow had was her kidneys.

Core Reasoning

As all this was going on, I was continuing my now-normal routine of addressing a core group of animals each day on my way home from work, unaware of anything abnormal (beyond me), and Gracie had become part of the group since Pop had come to visit. She never said much, but listened intently to all that went on. She was particularly interested in Bentley. Much later, I learned that a similar kind of bird had lived in the Gasparo household for many years and still resides with Mary's daughter. Mary says, "Gracie has met up with her equal when it comes to

Bentley. They are a match made in heaven. Who would have thought that a bird and a cat could become friends?"

I could tell, though, that on June 24th and a few days before, she'd not seemed to be herself. There was an unsettled air about her that I couldn't place right away. Now I recognize that "air" as something about to happen. Oddly, in my Open Session, it seemed as though she was two cats in one. I emailed Mary about it to ask questions.

She said of that time,

"Dinah sent me a email telling me that she had a strange session with her core group. Gracie had become a core member, but wasn't herself. She was like two cats in one. Dinah described Shadow. And by the way, I had not shared the Shadow story with Dinah yet. Dinah proceeded to ask me if I knew of anyone who'd lost a cat recently. That the cat who'd passed had given Gracie her kidneys, so Gracie could live. That is when I told Dinah about Shadow and Ann."

119

Then things seemed to fall into place in Mary's mind.

"For awhile after, Gracie didn't act like Gracie. You see, Gracie is a very stand offish. Suddenly, she was a very loving cat. Totally out of character. But, Shadow was a love bug. So for quite some time, I had two kitties in one."

So What's a Shadow Got to Do With It?

Of course, a blessing for one becomes grief for another. Ann, who had lost a life partner in her little Shadow, was grieving horribly. Not only did I need to get to the bottom of the kidney mystery and have a clearer understanding of what had happened, but I had a feeling that Shadow had a purpose on this earth that may not have been evident to those humans she'd come into contact with over the years. I had to understand that as well. This was a learning process for me.

I again, went to my guides for their help prior to calling Ann, who'd just gotten home from rehabilitation, never to see her loving cat again. I settled down and began my communications with the deceased Shadow. It was painful for me, but I'd learned a lot about the animal world and what kindness and love they are truly capable of.

In human terms, Shadow would be classified as a Saint. She had a purpose on earth that transcended human companionship and love. She was a healer. You've all heard of people who could heal with thought and with laying on of hands. This was a cat who was given this ability. Shadow, a stray, feral animal had lived a life of pain and suffering on the streets before her late years with Ann. But this suffering was one of choice, for she had helped many a sick and dying animal in her time. Shadow was one who would give life force to those needing it at the expense of her own life. She has saved many in her life on earth.

Ann was her reward for a job well done. In Ann's life was where she was to take her last stand. Loved by Ann. Mourned by Ann. Remembered by Ann.

Telling Ann all these things was not easy. It was a tearful unloading of emotion. The bright side—though it would be some time before things looked bright for Ann—was that Shadow, in our communication, had advised that once she'd had the opportunity to heal herself on the other side, she would be ready to reincarnate into another kitten and become part of Ann's family again. I was told that Ann and Mary were to keep an eye out—they would know the right time, the right place, and the right kitty.

Relaying the urgency at the time of Shadow's passing was difficult, but Ann needed to know that a conversation and agreement had been made between Gracie and Shadow. Shadow felt so very badly that the time of passing came when Ann was not at home, but there was no time to spare. She wanted me to convince Ann that it was okay that she was not there at Shadow's end—it was her time to go and the right time. She needed to "step up to the plate" and she wanted Ann to be proud of her for helping Gracie.

Ann *was* so proud.

As for Gracie, Mary has difficulty putting into words how grateful she is to Shadow for her sacrifice to keep her beloved cat alive, nor can she even *begin* to extend herself to Ann for her sacrifice of losing the precious Shadow in one last grand stand of giving.

In May, 2009, Gracie is still going strong, healthy, and living a normal life. I talk to her and two other cats belonging to Mary on a daily basis. Mary says: "It's funny, I can always tell when you have one of your sessions. Gracie always comes back with that extra skip in her walk as her tail wags back and forth."

And the gift to me is that Gracie is now part of my core group. *Some*body had to keep Bentley on his toes.

Another Shadow

Once Ann's Shadow had passed and Gracie was on her way to a healthier life, a new shadow came to reside at Mary's house. This one, though, was not an animal—at least I don't think it was. This one was a real-live-swirling-ghostlike shadow; the kind one might (or might not) see in an actual ghost investigation.

And it was under the bed in Mary's grown son's room.

But I believe I'm getting ahead of myself. Before anyone knew of the shadow, the door to the shadow's room was opening all by itself. Mary would close it securely, but still, she would always find it open when she walked by.

At first, though she'd mentioned it to me, she took it in stride. We were, after all, participants in a ghost group and wasn't it apropos for doors to open and close on their own in our houses? But when she saw it happen herself, her feelings intensified.

Setting up a camera, as any good ghost hunter would do, she managed to catch the scene on video. What was opening this door? She was on a mission to solve the mystery.

Furthermore, someone else had witnessed this strange door-opening ritual, and was caught on tape. Lilly had seen it and was prominently featured in the video, stepping back quickly and on high alert as the door flew open. She was definitely seeing something other than the door.

Lilly, Mary's white-with-black-spots cat was the first to see the churning mass beneath the bed, too. I learned this one afternoon when I was questioning Gracie about the opening door. In the next moment, Lilly was there talking to me. This was the first time I'd met Lilly and was surprised to see how my guide, the Lemur, was taking to her. As I talked to her, the Lemur was carrying Lilly around in his arms as she purred contentedly. Lilly was definitely more interested in my guide than me, but she still answered questions. Our session went like this:

"So what's opening the door, Lilly?" I asked.

"My goodness, you're dense this morning! Pop is here…but he's not here. He's just checking in on Mom. You know she's been walking with sticks. [Then I got the impression of a single stick as opposed to plural. Note: Mary was using a crutch to get around due to an injury.] He wants Mom to look under the bed." She was matter of fact and was obviously enjoying the attentions of the Lemur.

"What will she see if she looks under the bed?" I asked.

"A small shadow. Not a bad one. But it does annoy me."

She apparently had seen the shadow after Mary's son's bedroom door flew open. It was a little puff of smoke type thing and was under his bed. A thoughtform came to my mind. A thoughtform, according to demonologist Katie Boyd, is "a type of negative energy created from a single or group of people's emotions and thoughts. Usually created during times of argument, depression, stress, or all of these emotions at once." She also mentions that thoughtforms can appear as dark clouds. It is an extension of a person.

Lilly was a "pet" of my animal guide, the Lemur. He enjoyed carrying her around as she talked in the Core Group meeting one afternoon. Lilly is the cat who first saw the shadow beneath the bed at Mary's house. *Photo courtesy of Mary Gasparo.*

Lilly continued, "Get it out in the open so it can go away. Best thing for it. Shadow [Ann's deceased cat] doesn't need that kind of nonsense now."

This session ended with Lilly showing me that her coloring was the same as my own deceased dog, Tessa—black and white.

Lilly said, "Isn't it pretty?"

I agreed that, indeed it was. She also told me that I needed counseling for my own cat, since he doesn't seem to like me as much as she [Lilly] does. This was so true. My Murphy O'Reilley was a snooty cat towards me.

When I made the attempt to look under the bed during the session, my guides allowed it, as this was apparently something that was affecting the animals in the house. I felt certain that Lilly didn't know what the shadow was. But she knew it was there and was concerned about Shadow, the deceased neighbor's cat, and that *this* shadow would be a problem. I could not

figure out why this would be a problem—other than as a stressor for Gracie, who Shadow was now intricately connected with. But the thought was there.

My personal vision of the shadow was a swirling kind of black and gray smoke. But it wasn't swirling a lot; it was just hovering right above the floor, not even aware that I or Lilly was looking at it. I didn't have any feelings about it at all. All I knew for sure was that it was in the room, that Pop wanted the door open, and that Lilly thought it would go away if the door was kept open.

When telling Mary, though, I cautioned her because cats don't have a concept of the reality of the mixing of the here-and-now and the beyond. I told her to be careful because this bed shadow might be picking up strength. It might become bigger or turn into something more menacing. Still, having Mary's father around to keep an eye on things seemed to be a good thing at the time.

All this most certainly had something to do with the mystery, Mary thought, but now in addition to an opening door, she had a shadow under the bed. We both thought it was time to call in the big guns as this shadow and door opener was beyond what I, as an new animal communicator, could really deal with. So the next call went out to psychic medium Laurie Hull.

Laurie, the director of Delaware County Ghost Research was no stranger to shadows, spirits, and strange goings-on and was only too happy to be part of the investigation. Shadows were right up her ghostly alley. Upon tuning in to the situation, more information came to light: She felt that there was a male spirit there, one that Mary's son brought home from his line of work as a policeman. The spirit had been killed or murdered and had at some point latched onto Mary's son. Apparently, his death was never solved and he felt it would help his family to know who killed him and how his death occurred. Laurie advised that Mary needed to help him realize that it wasn't necessary for him to stay for this reason and that he needed to cross over to the other side to find peace. Then he would be able to help his family. Laurie felt, as I did, that this was not a mean or negative spirit, just one that needed help.

Now, taking a step away from animals, but still within the confines of ghostly phenomena, let me say that Laurie and Mary were both involved in still more pieces of the earlier-mentioned dark investigation one night during this shadow incident at Mary's house. I was not left out, though I did not actively participate. The three of us began to have connected negative dreams: red eyes glowing in the dark, fits of nausea (often a sign of psychic phenomena), and physical discomforts. Mary was on crutches, Laurie lost a close relative and was plagued with dreams, I was sick for months with unidentifiable headaches. And there were other members in my own group suffering varied maladies as well, one seemingly critically at the time.

The Wiz Kid

We add now to the mix, Belle, a beautiful Calico, and another of "Mary's girls." This was another call for medical scrying, i.e., to see or predict the future of a medical mystery. Just like the last one, with Gracie, I was afraid of letting Mary down. (You know the drill: What if I'm wrong? What if, what if?) But I wasn't going to sit back if there was a possibility that I might be of assistance.

After Belle's surgery to be spayed, she developed a lump the size of an egg on her stomach. At first, the medical community advised that the lump was a reaction to her stitches. This happened sometimes, and she was advised that it would go away. But not only did it *not* go away, it got bigger. Further, she was peeing all over the house, something unusual for her. She'd even gained the moniker Wizzer because of this.

So when Mary asked, I went down into my meditation mode and contacted Belle. It was a quick conversation, but I was told that she was peeing to get the attention she needed for her Mommy to get her to the hospital—something needed to be done about the lump on her stomach. I saw a spongy-like material inside the lump when I tried to determine what it was. I didn't think it was going to get better

Belle had a mysterious lump on her belly and used a bad habit to get everyone's attenion. *Photo courtesy of Mary Gasparo.*

on its own. My feeling, though, was that it was not cancer.

Mary saw to it that she did have surgery and it turned out to be a soft tissue mass. She'd had a small hole in her incision and because of the allergic reaction to the original stitch material, her stomach was swollen from that original surgery. It made an inside stitch pop open, and tissue, fat etc., leaked through. Once the second surgery was complete and Belle was put on antibiotics, not only did the egg shrink and get well, but the wizzing around the house subsided. Unfortunately for Belle, though, the name Wizzer stuck.

Mary was happy because it was difficult to figure out Belle's problem. There'd been an X-ray, an ultra sound, and a biopsy to see what the lump was. The doctor conducted the surgery when Mary insisted on it after we discussed the "spongy-thing." So in

Belle is now a happy camper and is seen here enjoying a sunbeam. *Photo courtesy of Mary Gasparo.*

My conversation with Belle after her surgery went like this:

(She didn't mention pain at all.) She said, "Woohoo, I'm gonna get better!"

"So," I said, "does that mean you're going to stop peeing on the floor?"

"I had to let them know something was wrong somehow…and then keep letting them know."

So I advised her to use the litter box and sent her a picture of her pawing in the litter.

For those of you who are keeping tabs on the strange negative occurrences happening since the ghost group took on the dark and dismal case:

🐾 Hospitalization of Gracie with failing kidneys (Saint Shadow to the rescue)

🐾 Death of Ann's cat, Shadow

🐾 Ghostly shadow under the bed at Mary's home, possibly identified as the spirit of a murder victim

this case, though the amount of information I could provide was scant, it was enough to make a decision to go further with the medical community. And this was what was needed.

🐾 Several sick investigators (and their family members)

🐾 A sickly Belle

Thinking about all that had happened over the last months, while the group was involved with the dark investigation, I had to voice my opinions to Mary. My gut said that she needed to stay far away from the case, because something knew way too much about her life and what was important to her. When others around her became involved too deeply with her, things began happening in their households, too. Each incident went to the heart of the person attacked. I felt that if there *was* to be a positive thing, it would become evident, but that for now, things had gone beyond weird and had affected her at her deepest emotional level—her cats.

It was time to give up the ghost, so to speak, so that others with more experience with possession, demonology, and negative spirits could take the lead. I, for one, wanted no part of it.

Connection? Maybe. We think so. Regardless, a reason to always be careful whenever involved with such things. Let the professionals handle it.

6. A Horse is a Horse
Of Course, of Course — Solo

"Animals do not usually seem surprised when they are contacted telepathically. They are often delighted that they can finally be understood. After all, they have understood us for ages..."

~Anita Curtis

That day in training at the Anita Curtis workshop, I was exposed to many varied individuals with numerous pets (dead and alive), all wanting to learn to communicate with animals. Everyone had a different reason. Some were there to connect with a deceased animal in an effort to reduce the mourning and agony of loss. Some wanted to be able to nip bad behaviors in the bud. Others needed to know any variety of things about the animals they worked around, or lived with, from medical issues to daily maintenance matters. I was the only one there writing a book. Yet I could identify with each person, for you see, I had a deceased dog, an ill dog, a cat with an attitude, I worked with animals, I lived with them, and I loved them.

On the second day of the classes, we were ready to sit in pairs to practice communicating with each other's animals. This was exciting. I'd heard people in the class talking about their dogs and cats and I was ready! I sat down in front of Gerri Gassert and she handed me her photograph. This then would be my very first animal communication. I gulped and my heart went to my throat.

It was a horse. I knew next to nothing about horses. The last time I'd been around one had been when I was ten and a little scout pony ran away with me—to this day, I can still see my father and uncle jumping fences with single bounds yelling at me to just let go and fall off.

Turmoil filled me. A horse.

His name was Solo.

I went through my meditation ritual as Anita had instructed, and in my mind's eye, I saw him—a magnificent creature, tall and beautiful. I identified myself as taught to do and said hello, telling Solo why I was there.

He said, "You've got to be kidding."

I was shocked. This had to be wrong. My heart began to beat fast and I started sweating.

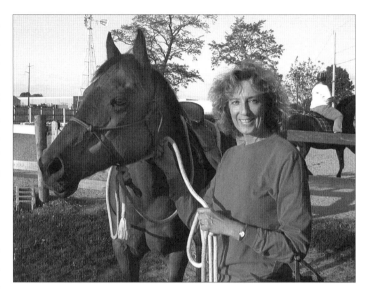

Solo continued, "You're terrible at this."

I tried to calm myself as I watched the horse watching me. Suddenly, I began to feel a small sensation—pins and needles sort of; that's as close as I can describe—in my fingertips on my left hand. Gerri told me that Solo did indeed have a hoof problem on the front left foot. Wow. I could do this, I thought.

But by now, Solo had had enough. He decided that it was his turn to diagnose me.

"Step inside me," he ordered.

This was an "invitation" to move into the animal as Anita had trained us to do with our guides. We could then experience what the animal was feeling. A bit apprehensive, in my mind, I took a step to the left and into Solo.

I was surprised at what I saw. I was aware that I was wearing huge Elton John-type sunglasses that had pink glass—that is, Solo was wearing them. I was ready to laugh, but he nudged me with—well with something…not sure what, but I stopped the need to giggle.

"This," he said with a sarcastic tone, "is the way you see the world."

I looked out through the big sunglasses with rose-colored lenses. The field beyond was pinkish red as was everything in sight. I frowned.

Solo repeated his thought. "This is the way you see the world."

Then he popped up the lenses so that everything was normal. He said, "*This* is the way it really looks!"

When I told Gerri what I was seeing, she asked me if I looked at the world through rose-colored glasses? I was ready to say no, but then I stopped to think. Solo was right. I did look through rose-colored glasses. I'd never thought that it was a bad or wrong thing; it was my personality. But it wasn't how things really were in many cases.

This I learned from a horse. (I also learned that horses have fabulous senses of humor.) As far as I was concerned, I'd made a friend. He'd told me how it was.

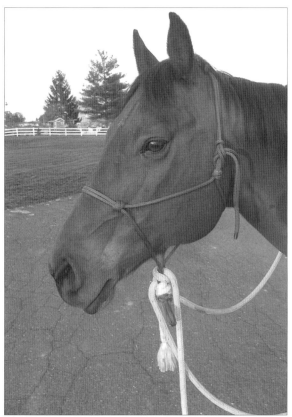

And Gerri reciprocated by letting me know that Murphy, my cat, didn't eat his food because he only wanted salmon for the wet food. I thought that might be boring, just having one kind of food day in and day out so I'd been giving him different meals everyday per my own tastes. She gave the example of having ice cream everyday after dinner—how nice would that be? This was how Murphy felt. So I now feed him salmon and he loves it. If I try to slip in chicken, he snubs it—and me. Spoiled, yes? She also told me that he hates Rufus barking in his ears—Gerri felt it as her ears throbbing—something that Rufus did routinely at mealtime just so Murphy didn't get the idea that the food was all his.

But back to Solo. This horse was a barrel of laughs—or maybe I should say bucket. And he loves the fact that now Gerri can talk with him and share his chuckles. She shared a very funny story showing a very ornery Solo. In her words:

"I don't think I told you what Solo did to my mild-mannered friend who has a horse in the same barn. She and I

Solo was my very first reading during training—and he made sure that I knew how terrible I was at it! *Photo courtesy of Gerri Gassert.*

work together also (that came first), so we go to the barn on opposite nights so we can keep an eye on the horses each day. The barn family is very nice, but there's nothing quite like knowing a fellow 'Mom' is checking on things. Solo has always done things to her, like spread a grassy smear between her shoulders, try to scare her when she gives him a treat, snort gook all over her, etc." [I was thinking how much this sounded like Solo's sense of humor.]

"Well, about two weeks ago, she noticed his water bucket was near empty. She went out to fill up the bucket, which holds five gallons, and brought it to his stall. In the past, he has 'gotten' her by drinking the water as it pours from one bucket to another, then quickly flipping his nose at her and splashing her all over. [Yup, he's ornery.] She's on to that one, so when he stepped over and started drinking the water she quickly backed out of the stall, shut the door, and told him she wasn't coming back in till he swallowed the water in his mouth.

"She said she waited at least five minutes, finding pleasure in outlasting him. He kept looking at her, then finally started to shake his head up and down very quickly and flap his lips really loud. Horses can do that, it's hilarious. I'd never seen him do it before, and neither had she. It was as if he was telling her, 'Hey, it's gone. Really, see?'

"So she went back in and proceeded to fill his bucket. But the water no sooner started pouring than she felt his nose on the back of her neck, and a split second later— WHOOSH! He let go of all the water he still had in his mouth and drenched her back!! Can you believe he would be that calculating?" [Oh yes, I can believe it!]

If you remember me saying early on, I'd begun to write this book as part of a ghost book detailing the beautiful and haunted Lancaster County, Pennsylvania. But as I wrote, a totally different book took shape—the one you are reading now. So instead of putting up the pretense of actually writing a ghost book, I switched gears, gave the Lancaster ghost book up to my good friend, psychic Laurie Hull, who would roll my ghost stories into her haunted Pennsylvania book. It was my thought to concentrate on ghost animals.

But Solo was not entirely comfortable with the change. One day, he came to Open Session with a formal question.

"I assume I will have a part in this book?" he asked me in a most regal tone.

I was honest with him and told him that I didn't know just yet because not only hadn't I gotten that far, but I didn't know how his owner, Gerri, would feel about my using her name and his in a ghost book. He told me very matter-of-factly that the decision to use his name rested with him and that it was indeed okay; in fact, it was important to him. Despite his pressure, I still touched base with Gerri to get permissions.

At this time, too, he also let me know that "the bird" [Bentley] was *not* my first customer. It was him. And that *he* was the one who taught me about sarcasm in animals. Not the bird, he reiterated. I had to clarify that I meant Bentley was my first "customer" out in the world, but not my first training partner. He had trained me at Anita's workshop. He was okay with that, then. I also told him that I believed that the focus was really going to be more of a ghost book with animals from beyond. (Get this.) He told me he thought he could round up some dead horses and that he would intermediate conversations for me if I chose. Of course, as books go, I didn't need the dead horses—I had plenty of mysteries without stirring up more. But the fact that he offered, was a wonderful tribute.

It seems, too, that animals know more about sports than we may have initially (or ever!) believed.

Gerri was working at the barn one night and as she was leaving, he called out to her, "Hey, keep me posted on the Phillies will ya?"

She stopped dead in her tracks, not believing that she'd really heard Solo in her mind. She said pensively, "Okay, so you like baseball?"

He answered, "Yeah, I like baseball. They're winning right now I hear."

So she scurried out to the car to tune into the game, and sure enough, they were winning. Solo told another animal communicator that not only does he like sports, but that he can read and tell time. It cracked her up though, and she noted that her skill at communicating with animals had to be real because she wouldn't have thought to bring up something like that—so it had to be him!

Gerri's friend, also an animal communicator and intuitive, was the first to really talk to Solo. She advised Gerri that the reason he was so sarcastic was that he was tired of trying to "get through" and not being able to. After she spoke with him, his demeanor seemed to change and the difference was dramatic enough for everyone at the barn to notice. He went from being not-so-nice to sweetheart. But this is as long as he can get his point across. Gerri, feeling his impatience, and like me, having trouble talking to her own animal at times, decided to give

Anita Curtis a call. There was excitement in the barnyard! Anita wasn't some silly trainee like Gerri and me! Anita could hear specifics!

When Solo Speaks, The World Listens

Gerri was excited about her appointment with Anita and she confided to me that once the time was upon her, she'd never felt fifteen minutes go by so quickly. She could've spent the afternoon talking about her beautiful horse. She scribbled madly, trying to get down every single thing Anita told her.

At first, Anita made sure that it was Solo she was talking to. So to begin with, she talked about Solo's sensitive teeth and the small white areas on his hind legs. "Bingo!" said Gerri. This told her that Solo was "in the house."

Gerri's first question was: What does he most want me to know?

He wanted her to know that he realized that she talked to him constantly and that he liked that. What he *didn't* like so much was that when she asked her questions, and he answered very quickly, she would hear that answer in her mind, but would tend to dismiss it. [I felt sorry for her, because I knew the feeling well.] This made him angry—actually in his words:

"It $*&#@ me off!"—and he eventually shuts down.

Then further annoyance occurs when Gerri, not knowing that he's already answered, keeps asking the same questions over and over. He wanted her to trust that she was hearing him correctly the first time.

He also wanted her to know that he didn't get out enough and that this was unacceptable. Through Anita, Gerri explained to him that he was being boarded in a barn and that she couldn't help it. He advised that this was not his problem and that she needed to do something about it. [Yes, this was definitely Solo talking!]

On a sad note, he told Anita that he really missed the Paint Horse that used to be at the barn and asked if he was coming back. Gerri thought that he meant a horse by the name of Pistol, because they used to hang out together in the pasture. Solo also told her that he liked the big black horse to play with and that he was fun to push around—Gerri had seen just that during the prior week.

He does not like his new blanket at all. It came up too far on his neck—he'd rather have nothing at all if he wasn't going to have his old blanket.

Gerri was worried, as all animal lovers worry, was Solo having any pain?

He told Anita that it comes and goes, but no, nothing to worry about. He does not, he says, need the medication his vet says he needs. He's fine. [It's probably best not to make decisions based entirely on the animal saying that he does, or does not, need medication, but it's certainly something to discuss with your veterinarian if the topic comes up.]

Of course, being as spiritual as Gerri is, she wanted to know how many lifetimes Solo and she have had together.

The answer came quickly. Six. Gerri told me:

"In one, my name was Mildred and he was my Jack Russell. We lived in Mississippi in the '20s. I was not prim or proper and he loved that. That was a fun life. We were also husband and wife in pioneer days, taking our children across the prairie in a wagon train. We didn't make it to our destination. In that lifetime I was old beyond my years and I didn't talk to him the whole way because I didn't want to go. I was always cold (still am this time around, too, he said!) and had gnarled hands. More recently, I was a young man who liked to fly planes and he was my horse. (This is interesting. In past readings I was told that we were human brothers, and son/mother, so that might account for a few more lives!)"

Gerri's next question: Would he like it if she had her own farm to keep him with her?

"Absolutely! Yes!" was his quick response.

And he would like to have Katie back (a little pony that used to be next to him in the stall).

"He says that we have to get her back when we have a place," said Gerri.

Anita told him that the pony's spirit may have left her body by then, and he said he knew this, "but if that's the case, she'll come back to us."

This was truly amazing to Gerri because this pony had been the first horse she was sure she'd heard talk to her. Solo said that the pony had been with them before and wants to come back to them again.

Very recently, Gerri told me that a strange cat had shown up at the barn and has stayed on—Nickers was his name. It was an odd arrival. Gerri asked, "Did Nicky come to the barn for me?"

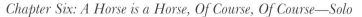

Solo advised that "Nick" had been on the wagon train with them in a past life. He had found his freedom; he didn't like living in a house and being shut in.

He escaped and ran, and when he saw Solo, he said, "Wow! You're here, too? I'm staying!"

Nick the cat is now a barn familiar, having traveled with Solo and Gerri in a past life on a wagon train headed for the wild west. *Photo courtesy of Gerri Gassert.*

He loves the freedom of living in the barn. So now there is a new family barn member.

I'd asked Gerri to find out from Anita what Solo wanted his readers to know since he was going to be a major part of my book.

She told me:

"He wants everyone to know how intelligent he is, and Anita seconded that—she said he is a horse with a head on his shoulders. He is not a guide for me in this life, but he is ahead of me in terms of soul evolution. He has learned more than I have. He said all you have to do is ask, 'Who has to work to keep who?'"

And I, of course, pass on to you that this is a smart horse. I'm finding, too, that horses in general have a real wit and charm about them that often surpasses other animals. They truly look at us at an equal level and expect to be treated as such. They do, however, understand their positions along their life travels.

Just a Job, Not a Career

…which brings to mind the story that started my path down the animal communications lane—the Amish horse that had dropped dead from exertion in Paradise, Pennsylvania. That long ago day that I cried myself all the way home and poured out letters of animal abuse to every place I could think of never really left my mind. It was a reason to learn this skill. But it was quite some time before I could revisit that day in my mind. That was a day filled with horror and pain. It had to be done sooner or later, but I'd pushed it away. How could I make up for the dreadfulness heaped on this kind soul? But the time was now.

Stealing away to an empty room in my home, locking out the barking dogs and my husband, who I'm sure thinks I'm crazy most of the time, I settled down in a rocking chair. Taking deep breaths, I moved into the meditative state that would allow me to call out to the universe to a horse that I did not know. Was it a male or female? Did it have a name? How would I recognize it and would it recognize that this strange woman wanted to talk about times past?

My own spirit guides glanced up at me as I made my way along the path. They were basking in sunshine and apparently did not feel the need to move. A second later, I saw why. A beautiful black horse stood on the path. There were no reins or harnesses encumbering it now. The sheen of the horse's coat reflected the light like glass. A magnificent creature.

I walked forward and explained who I was.

I received an interior nod and a question was posed to me in my mind as to why I would want to talk with him at this late date. Without waiting for my answer, the horse went on to say that he would talk with me. And without the question he said:

"Death was a release."

**Amish buggies with horses are familiar sights in Lancaster County, Pennsylvania.
These beautiful horses feel that they have an important job.**

It was said with such finality, but there was no remorse or sadness. It was stated as fact.

Were you abused? I asked in my mind.

"No, not really. This was a job. My job. It has been like this in my family for a very long time. It was what was needed to be done. I was responsible for transportation

140

on all days—hot or cold. And it was what I did. I do not feel badly about my death."

Are you happy now? I asked.

"Yes, though I sometimes miss the job. I have a job here, too, but I do not wish to talk about it with you." (This disappointed me, because I truly wanted to hear—right from the horse's mouth so to speak—what it was like on the other side for him.)

"Do not mourn me or my life," he continued. "It was fine. It was my job."

And then he was gone. This was strange. I'd not been prepared for his words. I'd been ready to throw myself at his mercy, hoping that he would recognize that not all humans were so cruel to their animals. Oddly, I almost felt cheated. I still felt that he deserved a vengeance of some kind, but that was not the way of the world, nor the way he saw it.

A Hard Horse to Kick

Hearing what the Amish horse had to say, helped somewhat, but I must say that I still call out a blessing to every one I see pulling a buggy in whatever weather condition. I worry about them. I never can tell if they hear me or know that I'm caring for them, but I send out the love anyway. Just in case there's a way for blessings to really get to the animals (or people) I send them.

I was at the market one afternoon recently, and the day was cold, but not horribly so—it was just a chilly day. I was leaving the parking lot in my car and stopped at a red light. Suddenly, up next to me, pulls an Amish buggy led by a beautiful beige horse. I tensed. The buggy was close to me and looking to my left out the window I could see the horse ever so near. He was strapped into a pulling contraption (you can tell I know little about horses) and had blinders on.

My heart ached for him and I sent him a blessing in my head. Suddenly, I saw from peripheral vision, him stamp his feet and turn his head in my direction. *Wow, he heard me*, I thought. I quickly went into animal communications mode and sent him a loving greeting. He again threw his head toward me.

The Amish driver of the buggy began to pull at the reins to pull his head back straight, but the horse was having none of it. Finally, the horse managed to turn his head to stare directly into my car window and into my eyes. He was no further than two feet from me. I could see the chilled air smoke from his nose as he snorted and he nodded up and down three times. It was a nod to me, accepting my greeting and offering his own.

I glanced up at the Amish man who was frowning and struggling to pull the horse's head back. Anger touched me for a second or so, but then it fled as the horse stamped his front foot again, drawing me back.

In my head, I heard, "Greetings, my friend. Joy to you."

I returned, "Joy to you as well, my friend."

The light turned green and we parted ways. Horses are wonderful creatures.

I suppose this is as good a time as any to make note that not all Amish people abuse their animals, I'm told. I'd been over-exposed to the negative cases, and because of that, a small ping of anger erupts each time I see an animal in their stead. Animal abuse is, of course, found in all walks of life and not just in this one religious sector.

Still, feeling that rip in our fabric of consciousness keeps me on my toes. Someone has to step up and make a sound for fair and loving treatment of other sentient beings. I hereby stand.

7. The Block

"Mystery: any truth that is unknowable except by divine revelation."

"Block: A sudden cessation of speech or a thought process without an immediate observable cause, sometimes considered a consequence of repression. Also called mental block."

~Dictionary.com

I was no stranger to writer's block, which had attacked me in earlier years, but I'd learned that if I took charge of my brain by employing a simple method called clustering (or webbing in some teachings), this would dislodge the block and I'd be on my way to creative wonder. Once I'd tried this method, some twenty years prior, I'd not seen hide nor hair of true writer's block again.

I say "true" writer's block because there are other natural blocks that do not involve the creative thinking aspect of writing. If one is under difficult stress, extremely tired, or any other crazy thing that would require a shift of brain functions, a block might come. What I was feeling was not a writer's block, but rather a personal block of some kind. It was easy to identify. If the clustering/webbing did not work, then I knew that I'd have to employ some sort of personal reflection to determine what had me in its clutches. Why didn't I want to write? Once

discovering the why, then I would be on my way to getting back into the scribing groove. Either way, identification was not that difficult. Any supreme worry, whether it be related to money, family, work, illness—whatever—if I sat down to think about it, I could figure it out.

But when the animal communications block came, I was at a loss. This was new territory for me. There was no clustering needed to stimulate a deadened imagination. There was no underlying stress that I could identify. The skill was just gone.

Well, gone, might be a bit too dramatic. There were still small parts available to me, but they were a mystery without the clues, the nightmare of any writer.

It all began approximately two weeks before the 2008 presidential elections. One day, I was asked to contact a cat because there were severe and life threatening things going on in the kitty's life. I took my visualization elevator down to the Ground floor, but when the door opened, my core group of animals was not there. Neither were my spirit guides. I was shocked. This was strange, because usually, as soon as I opened the door, I was bombarded with welcomes and affections from my core group. And the guides were always happily there to greet me as well. This time, no one was there. I remember frowning in wonder. Where was everybody?

So I went back to the original routine, and sauntered down toward the ocean and took the left path past the roll-top desk that led to the forest. Still no one…

I walked back to the desk and went deeper into my initial routine, found the photo of the cat in question, and then walked back to the treeline to meet my guides. This time they were there, but all I saw were their backs walking back into the forest. I stood there for nearly a minute perplexed, and then finally, alone, brought myself back to the reality I knew.

Later, I tried again, and this time, all the animals in my core group and my guides were there when I opened the elevator doors, but no one was talking.

They all just stood there, looking first to me, then at each other, as if to say, "Well, now what do we do?"

I tried conversing, but no one answered. Looking in exasperation at my guides, I asked, "What's wrong here? Why won't they talk to me?"

The guides both shook their heads in a negative fashion and turned away.

I was blocked.

The scary thing was, that in my life outside the elevator, things were crazy, too. *I* was crazy. A feeling of doom had engulfed me—I just knew that something was about to happen in November, and this was so overpowering, I could barely stand it. Could it be the political climate of the United States in the highly controversial upcoming presidential election? Was that what was bothering me? A "knowing" came to me that it was not the elections and I felt that it had to do with something that would affect me personally.

Because in my job, as editor for the paranormal, I talked with many ghost-related people and psychics on a daily basis from all around the country, I began questioning them. Had they been having strange gloom and doom feelings? In every case, I heard that yes, something was afoot in the ethereal. The large majority of people I spoke with felt that the *something* we all felt had to do with earth changes. Others felt that the political engine had something to do with the gloom. A small group felt that an awakening would be taking place. (I really like this last idea.)

But the common phrase that kept hitting my ears was, "It's coming."

And I was seeing and hearing that phrase everywhere! It was on television shows, on people's lips, and my own mind was spewing it. I was becoming paranoid.

So what does one do when one becomes paranoid? I went to the Internet. (Okay, stop laughing. Stupid yes. But I needed to do the research.)

Paranoia Sets In

Of course, there's no better place to increase paranoia than the Internet. It didn't take very long to tune me into all the prophesies of 2012—December 21st to be exact. It was interesting that all the things I was considering—earth changes, politics, terrorism—figured prominently. Now, I'd heard, of course, of the varied themes around this end-of-the-world sentiment. I'd watched the documentaries on television relating to the Mayans, the Bible Code, the UFO phenomena, the afterlife, *Left Behind* book series, and every other kind of thing that was dumped in the *end of times* dumping ground. After all, this kind of topic was right up my ghostly alley. But now that I'd connected the dots of paranoia, things became pretty much overwhelming—and muddy.

Meanwhile, I kept trying to communicate with the animals and using my pendulum more and more to try to determine what the problem was and whether any of these things connected in reality. Furthermore, though I tried to keep it at bay, there was a little anger creeping into my quest because I couldn't figure out what was going on and no one in my core group would help. They'd deserted me.

The elections came and went. There were no great or horrendous events. Though one psychic friend who has been able to see the face of the new president every election *prior to* the election, saw only a blank face this year. And even after the election, the face remained blank in her psychic mind. That could not be good. (Later, after the fact, I still worry about this one.)

Then there came a small victory—or breakthrough might be a better word. Thank God for little Bentley. I'd tried not to vary my routine of communications, and everyday on the way home from work, I kept trying to have my Open Session. I'd always see the animals sitting there, but not talking. It was like a kindergarten class waiting for the teacher to make a great proclamation that involved some wicked end—like no recess.

I was rapidly becoming a basket case. The latest news I'd heard from a reliable psychic source, was that the words, "It's coming," had been heard in a clairaudient fashion—that is, power to hear things outside the range of normal perception. So I wanted to know, just what the hell was coming and why couldn't I talk to the animals? Did it affect just me or was it a world thing?

As I opened the elevator door that afternoon, the animals were again just *there*—doing nothing but watching me. I implored the guides that they be allowed to talk with me but my leopard just shook his head no—even he was not speaking. Then ever so cautiously, with a fearful glance at my guides, little Bentley stepped forward. He was nervous—not a trait that anyone could attribute to this proud little bird. He said, "We're not allowed to talk to you." Then he stepped back in the line like a private in the army during inspection. The guides were glaring at him. I saw a mental shrug from the bird as if to say, "Someone had to tell her."

A "knowing" came to my mind immediately—I'm not sure it was from Bentley, but I expect so. The thought was that there was something that I was not to know and that there was the fear that the animals would tell me—because they *wanted* to tell me big-time. And the fact that they had the same kind of free will that we had meant that somehow they had to be silenced.

I did my best to go on with my life, but I admit to making those around me paranoid, including my husband who has now been convinced to sit on the 2012 band wagon with me. The old "what if" (which is a writer's thing) works as well in reality as it does in imagination.

To make matters worse, Bentley's unintentional sidekick, Pipsqueak, had taken to thinking that in order to be in this book, her contributions had to keep on coming. My guides did relate to me that Pips wanted to tell what shouldn't be told. (Do you see why I feel crazy with this world-inside-my-world interactions?)

Anyway, once the elections were over and I still hadn't regained my ability, the feelings of doom

persisted, actually increased. So much so that I was certain that by Thanksgiving, I might not ever see anyone again. I felt death, I felt inability to affect change, I felt totally down. I was a zombie waiting for the worst, even going so far as to tell my parents that if something happened and I never saw them again, that I loved them. I was going bonkers.

This feeling was intensified as I tried to use my pendulum. The practice hooks to my higher self committee, which includes guides, angels, my higher self (soul), and varied departed relatives. Most all my questions were, as usual, eagerly answered—except when I asked anything about my animal communications, 2012, my feelings of current doom, earth changes, or anything that affected terrorism. (They don't like lottery questions either, but I'd learned that early on.) Instead of swinging wide as usual, the pendulum would stay still and then shake as if there was a struggle in the world beyond regarding how, if, or who, should answer.

A World Crisis

Then the Mumbai attacks occurred in India— being called India's 9/11. This was a major world crisis. Almost immediately after this horrible event, I began to feel a tad better and the gloom slowly started to lift—a little. But very little. Was this India event the tragedy that I'd been fearing?

It took me back to the days prior to 9/11 in New York and at the Pentagon. At that time, though very interested in the paranormal, I was not as savvy in any ability sense. Days before the attacks, I'd felt out of sorts, moody, and not in a good state of mind. I'd paced a lot. Thinking of the old movie, *Star Wars*, I correlate that feeling now to something being wrong in "the force." And it was. The world suffered because of it.

My feelings weren't as pronounced then as now because in this time I'd been exercising that part of my brain that gives psychic awareness. Then, I was merely part of the "normal" unenlightened world order, just plodding along like so many lost sheep.

The interesting part was that this particular incident in India did not seem to have a connection to my world of animal communication, unless one took into consideration that for the guides to shut me down because the animals might tell me something, lends credence to our animals' abilities to not only know the future, but to respond to it prior to its occurrence. This brings to mind how animals can be seen running from disaster long before we humans have a clue that "it's coming." Just how deep does their "knowing" go?

When December of 2008 rolled around, my doom and gloom had subsided quite a bit—but not all the way. It was as if things were not quite done. There was another blow to be endured. The animals were still not talking to me. It was then that another psychic medium I trusted, Beckah Boyd, reminded me that maybe there were other things at play that were blocking me. She mentioned stress and worry (if I was feeling either, I didn't recognize it), poor

diet (hmmm… this was true, but my diet was no different now than when the animals *were* talking to me), and any number of things that could affect my personal aura. She advised me that it could be a personal thing. In fact, it probably *was* a personal issue for me.

Bottom line, I was still at a loss, and continued to mourn my loss of skill and begged my higher being (God) to bring the talent back.

The newest variation came in the beginning of December. As I left the elevator on the Ground floor of my meditation, there was nothing but fog. This was new. There had never been fog before—except in the "future" building, which was to my left. The leopard was there but he would not speak—he just nodded and shook his head to answer my questions, making this a *yes-and-no* survey. And that can be so aggravating, especially when one doesn't know the right questions to ask. There was still something coming, but apparently, it would be for my good. Or if not *my* good, *somebody's* good. Of course, knowing that moving

to the next world is always thought of by those on the other side as a good thing, that worried me. Was God's good my good? Frustrated still by the lack of communication, I found myself grimacing as I was getting my *yes and no* answers.

Suddenly, as though pulling a curtain open, Bentley stuck his little head out of the fog, looked at me, glanced at the leopard and then retreated behind the wall of fog again. Dear Bentley. Ever the eavesdropper. I knew he was dying to control the situation, but knew which side his bird bread was buttered on.

I did take a moment though to ask my guide for a favor, since I'd heard from Marla that there was again trouble in the bird cage of Hollywood. "I know that I'm not supposed to be talking to the animals, but could you please ask Bentley not to peck himself. He's upset by all this and I don't want him to be hurt because he can't participate in his group." The leopard nodded.

So, basically, I was still in the dark. I hoped Bentley would stop pecking.

Marla's email to me about Bentley in early December was disturbing and struck a negative cord with me. The paranoia was again rising. She said:

"All I can say is that Bentley is pecking less, but demands attention at night. He screeches up a storm till I go to him, but continues to screech loudly for several minutes even after I'm there." The bird was driving everyone around him crazy.

She continued, "He used to be fine in the bedroom with Pipsqueak and let me watch TV in my office till at least midnight. Now he's starting to complain loudly around 11pm. Last night, I brought his cage into the office and set it right next to me and he still didn't hush up. He's starting to do it in the afternoons, too, at least once a day."

It was obvious to me that something was escalating and it was affecting Bentley in a harsh way.

"I get the feeling," said Marla, "that it's not so much attention he craves, but since he can't talk to you, he's frustrated because it seems he definitely has something to say and is hoping I can read his mind…"

And so December moved forward. People I knew were most assuredly getting tired of my doom and gloom and *something's coming* mentality, so I began to stay quiet about it. Whatever happened would happen. But to be on the safe side, I'd begun stocking canned food in my spare bedroom and filling empty milk jugs with water—just in case the world was coming to an end. And I made sure that my husband knew that if I died—and he didn't— I wanted to either be cremated or to donate my body to science. I was serious.

Unwelcome Answers

On Wednesday, December 17, 2008, the sickness began. Nausea, inability to think, pacing, sleeplessness, loss of appetite…was I getting the flu? Something was always going around at work, so I started treating myself with over-the-counter drugs for colds and flu. I went to work, of course, and stayed securely in my office, interacting with as few people as possible—but this was out of mood more than anything else. I was grouchy as hell. I hid it, but did mention that I didn't feel very well. That usually kept people away.

At home that night, I couldn't sleep and the nausea increased. Thursday at work was more of the same, but I made it through. By Friday morning, I was seriously considering calling off sick, but knew that I had some important projects that had to be completed and that I had to go in to the office.

It was then that my guides came to me. Now these were not my animal guides, rather the tall tubes of white light that resided on the first floor of my elevator world.

Clearly in my head I heard, "You may go into work, but you must leave by twelve o'clock."

I frowned. Was that just me rationalizing why I should go to work sick and then leave early? But no, the voice had not been mine, but rather that strange "knowing"—yet this time with words. I went to work.

I was very nauseous all morning, but worked steadily. I went to meetings, I prepared books, I conducted my normal routines. I didn't throw up on anyone.

I had particular fun handing off a book to the design department about animals in the afterlife. Sitting in the publisher's office with the designer, we chatted about the vision of the book. Peter Schiffer, the publisher, my boss, friend, and a mentor, tried to offer his help to me as I explained my vision of heartwarming and loving feelings for the book to the designer. We were all laughing. It was a meeting I truly enjoyed and I left smiling, the nausea forgotten for a bit. Ah, animals.

Several times through the morning, I was reminded by a voice in my head coming from the guides that I needed to leave by twelve. It was so persistent, that it became a nuisance thought.

As time does, it got away from me. It was 3pm and I was finally packing up my things to leave—I was still leaving early, so the guides should be happy. The nausea was nearly a disability by now. I felt as though I was going to throw up any moment.

I said my good-byes to the people in the office, noticing that Peter was not in his office, though I'd just had a meeting with him not more than a few minutes before.

As I pulled out of the driveway, two ambulances rushed in.

The worst had happened. My wonderful boss, Peter Schiffer, died of a heart attack in the ambulance on the way to the hospital that day. A sudden ripping of the fabric of the world, of my world. I was not prepared for this tragedy.

Oddly, my blanket of coming doom, the nausea, and the paranoia lifted as though a bedspread had been pulled easily off a bed. This had been the "it" that had been coming for me. There was no question. It had all been about this tremendous personal loss of someone whom I'd cherished in life. The paranoia was now gone, to be replaced with terrible grief and questions of *why?*

The animals in my core group came rushing back at that moment, not even waiting until I called the elevator, but into my head like a shot. My departed Tessa was licking the tears from my face and Bentley was on my shoulder, whispering, "You'll be okay, you'll be okay, you'll be okay," over and over and over. Mary's three cats spoke in a single voice assuring me that, "He is okay. He is better now than when he was here." Solo just hung his head as if understanding my pain.

Knowing all that, of course, didn't helped with the grief in the days that followed. My thoughts finally went from my personal sorrow to Peter's family, and then more grief came, as I suffered that they should have to go through such a loss.

So with tears, I moved on. Peter Schiffer gone. It couldn't be, but it was. He would be missed in my life—and in the lives of all those around him, who loved and respected him.

A Block Epilog

The block was gone. The veil was lifted.

Looking back, I am surprised that I didn't remember the day my grandmother was murdered many years prior, when my feelings took a similar turn. There were no animals communicating at that time to amplify the issues, but the warning of doom had been much the same. It took me a long time to get over that event; and I'm sure that it will be the same now—as I've again lost someone important.

Now I understood why my guides had wanted me out and away from the office by twelve. They were taking precautions to protect me from a scene that would stay in my mind forevermore—that of

ambulances and the terror of what would happen next. I was supposed to find out *after the fact* and not in the fashion that ultimately occurred. They were trying to protect me.

I wonder now whether I'd have wanted to know prior to…would I have wanted the animals to tell me what was coming? Could I have changed anything? I think not, for if anything, this has reinforced the notion that while we have free will and can affect some things, there are experiences (such as death) that are not up for our control. Still, surprise is maddening and I would have liked to let Peter know how much I cared for him and how thankful I was that he was in my life. I'd never done that.

The animals took it easy on me those following weeks and I didn't solve any animal-related mysteries during that time. It seemed that my dear Cooneys had gone for the time-being, no doubt out doing the good work and spending holiday time around her former family, the D'Agostinos. I promised myself that I would check in with her soon, but I knew somehow that she'd moved on to her next assignment—I felt it. Solo the horse, too, was quiet, most likely back to green (or white with snow) pastures. I knew it would be a bit before things got back to normal.

Marla advised me that at her home in California, Bentley had been very "sullen" the prior few days—"not acting up, not being a brat." He had been very quiet, going to bed early and not making a sound. She said that he was acting just like he was in mourning. I believe he was. After all, we were all connected.

At any rate, a special co-worker sent me an email that had a quote from an unknown source. I'd heard it before, but now it fit perfectly.

They say it takes a minute to find a special person, an hour to appreciate them, a day to love them, but then an entire lifetime to forget them.

This holds true for both animals and people. I will never forget Peter Schiffer.

8. ITC Devices and Ghost Animals
The Rock Creature, Zira

"Could it be that through ITC devices that the consciousnesses of all communicators (spirits, ghosts, humans in-body) meet?"

~angelsghosts.com/instrumental_transcommunication

As a member of the Chester County Paranormal Research Society at the time, some of the investigative techniques we used to study the paranormal involved electronic voice phenomena devices.

Mark Sarro, the founder of CCPRS, has extensive firsthand knowledge of all the technical "do-dads" that have become popular in the world of ghost hunting. I'm often amazed at how far things have come—and of how little I know. There are new and wonderful worlds of exploration going on, on the technical side of the paranormal field—and I'm very lucky to be a part of it from time to time.

What Is ITC?

Before my next story, you should probably understand just what ITC is—Instrumental Trans Communication. (I can hear you saying: *What?*) According to Mark,

155

"ITC is the parent of EVP [electronic voice phenomenon], video feedback, talking boards, pendulums, etc. Essentially, it's communication with the spirit realm by means of a device... by using a continuous sweep through the radio frequencies, creating a linear sweep. The basic principal is that by creating this sweep through the frequencies, you can create a RF (Radio Frequency) field that will facilitate communication with the spirit realm. How these devices vary from traditional EVP recordings are that when you conduct a standard EVP session using a digital or analog audio recorder; you would ask questions aloud while recording and usually you would not 'hear' any answers to your questions until playback, and for most investigators this would be post investigation. [This

Mark Sarro with his ITC (Intramental Trans Communication) equipment. Mark lives in a haunted house. *Photo courtesy of Carol Starr.*

method of communicating] is much different; when you ask a question, if there is someone there to communicate [a ghost or spirit], you will hear the answer in real time!"

To learn more about these devices and about the CCPRS (Chester County Paranormal Research Society), visit www.chestercountyprs.com.

Now why would you want to do that? Well, to begin with, Mark Sarro, at the time of this writing, lives in a very haunted house. In a room on the top floor of his home, he has set up the *ITC Lounge*, which records visual and audio activity of a ghostly nature within that particular room. This is being done to research the varied phenomena present there.

Much activity has been noted in that strange room, including knocking, visual sightings of ghost figures, squealing and moaning, and movement of furniture. For quite a while, this live feed went directly to the Internet, which allowed viewers across the world to peek at a real haunted environment. Though I must add that Mark disconnected the camera from time to time when things were too weird, as when a weather front approached. Sometimes weather intensified varied anomalies. This was for the public's protection because there have been people who have become sick—as this is one sign that a person is receptive to psychic or otherworldly interactions—after being exposed to the room. (So I guess this is as good a time as any to offer the warning that this kind of activity is not for everyone and that you should pursue ITC devices or ghost research at your own risk.) From time to time, you might be able to catch a glimpse of the experimental research on the Livestream website: www.livestream. com/itclounge, but there is uncertainty regarding the actual continuation of this feed due to the circumstances surrounding it. Still, my personal story remains.

An Evening Lounging About in the ITC Lounge

One particular evening, two other members in the group accompanied me and an outside guest, each viewing this room from our own homes connected to the ITC Lounge at Mark's house.

At first, we just chatted among ourselves in the way of most Internet chat rooms. But at the same time, we watched for any activity surfacing in the room. The left base of the wall was pointed out by one of the viewers (seen via Camera 1 when set to view the far wall and windows). There sat what appeared to be an animal that looked very much like a rat or a cat. Another person felt it looked like a raccoon. In reality, the face of the creature seemed to shift from one animal to the next. All watching could see a tail wrapped around the back end of the creature, much as a cat curls its appendage around itself. Though there was a bit of movement at the face level, due to the changes in the face, for the most part, this creature sat silently in the room and seemed oblivious to anything there, or to any of us.

Though not specifically proven by scientific research, this visual anomaly seemed ghostly in nature, and those of us looking at it felt certain that

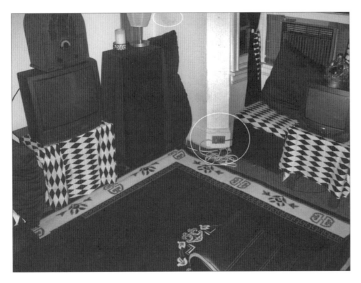

this was an animal ghost of some kind. I was asked by those in the group that night to go down into my meditation state to see if I could make contact to find out if this "animal" was really there and, if so, why it had come to reside in Mark's house. Mark had talked before of having a ghost cat in the house that sometimes slept with him, but this was different.

I was a bit worried because I'd certainly not gotten my full ability back since my guides had "shut me down" as discussed earlier, but I was willing to try. I needed practice to start over again.

Once I went down into my contemplation mode, I was able to make contact with "the creature." It surprised me. This was a very solemn creature, with no knowledge of its own being, of its location, or

The haunted room at Mark's house in West Chester, Pennsylvania. People have had any number of paranormal experiences here—not all of them good. Circled in this photo is an orb on the wall. Prior shots and those after this one did not show the orb. The other circle shown at the bottom of the wall is where the strange Rock Creature could be seen on live video feed. Its image did not show on the digital photo.

that it was visible to us in Mark's house. It had no thirst, no hunger, no sense of self. It had no name or knowledge of any kind.

I was given the sense that it was from a lower-level dimension. It was not from our dimension, but was fading through from another. This in itself is very disturbing, since it shows the possibility of a portal, which brings through not only good things, but evil or unwelcome things as well. If nothing else from the portal in Hollywood, I'd learned that control of such things was questionable. I became worried about the creature since it seemed to have no personality of its own, but only a shifting face of several animals.

Scrying for Animals

I pulled out my pendulum to do a program clearing for the creature in an effort to help it in any way that I could. Clearing actual programs is different than traditional cleansings used by most paranormal investigators and psychics and one I learned through the teachings of Robert E. Detzler in his book, *The Freedom Path*. [I must admit I have much more work to do in this area.]

Cleansings usually encompass an area, clearing said area of negative influences and spirits—it can be dangerous. Clearing *programs* do not clean an area or interact with negative influences, rather they clear the person of programs that they

This is an artist rendering depicting loosely what we saw when we were looking at the Rock Creature. Its animal features switched, it seemed, from cat to rat to racoon to fox.

are destined to run life to life until they "get it right." For example: A program running through one person's life might be that of abuse. Until that person learns the lesson required of the abusive situation, that program is run over and over again in each lifetime until it *is* learned.

So, if I am allowed to clear a program (the guides must give permission), that clearing takes a great lift off someone's karma and that person has a stronger aura because of it. This enables them to better handle other situations in their lives.

Now I cannot just clear a program without solving the issue at hand, and some programs take hours to clear. Others are quick and easy and require no research. These programs that require no research are the ones I clear. It makes that being/animal/human/creature stronger in the *now*.

This, too, was a time that I saw in action the importance of putting protections in place prior to using such a tool as the pendulum—or even being in the proximity of a room such as the one where the creature alternately (and supposedly) resided. The danger of not placing protection is that you will have no way of telling who will be answering your questions—especially, for us that night, since the house we were viewing was so haunted.

After learning the pendulum technique at an earlier juncture, I found that my personal protective spirits—my high-spirit committee—give the most reliable answers during my investigations, though, I've interacted with some spirit energy directly when my guides deem it safe. The strongest responses—and the most believable—come from those who protect me. So, though I wanted to help this creature by clearing away any negative energies around it, I needed to be very careful, because it was not the only energy in the room. I needed to focus on it alone.

As I was working with it, one of the other members in the room saw something run across the carpet close to the creature and asked that I try to contact that creature as well. They thought it was a ghost rat. So, once I'd finished clearing the creature's programs, I went down into my meditation state again. But, immediately, I realized that it was not a rat. It appeared to be a very large insect, and as I reached out to talk with it, it turned its head back at me with a very toothy snarl—nasty monster teeth for a little bug like this. Although when I say little, it was the size of a rat with a much bigger teeth. I got the impression right away of "leave me alone" in a snarl. So I backed away quickly and it ran on. This little guy has gotten a reputation now of being called the toothy roach by those of us who were witness that evening. It's not been seen again.

Still Haunting After All These Years

For a time, each Sunday night, Mark hosted a radio show called *Voices Carry* on Para-X Radio. His show not only took into consideration things that were going on in that haunted room, but talked about all the varied electronic devices for ghost hunting as well. In the past, to support the group and the show, many of the CCPRS members found themselves in the chat area watching the activity of the room and talking among themselves as things of a supernatural persuasion occurred (or not). The night after we first saw the creature, a new radio show was scheduled and we all arrived at the appointed time via the Internet to the ITC Lounge.

Right away, we saw that the creature was still there and had not moved—aside from the few movements of change taking place on the face from rat to cat to raccoon. (Was this a camera or pixilation issue? Had I really connected to this creature? Again, I questioned everything.)

As Mark's show progressed, he began using the Paranormal Puck (an ITC device that, hooked to a computer, types and recites words that are captured in the energy of the air at a particular location where set up) and the ITC machine by asking questions of the room. Several times, he asked, "Who is in the room?" The words coming across through ITC and the Paranormal Puck, repeated many times, were: *rock, world, rocks.*

It was then I got the distinct communication that the creature that I had been viewing from the lower dimension (my impression was "second level" though I hadn't a clue what that meant at the time) was not an animal at all. Rather, it was a rock. I suddenly knew that this creature from a lower dimension was slated to be an animal (rat, raccoon, cat?) in the future in another dimension. Some animals began as rocks, I was given, and they moved up. This came to me as a *knowing*. I can't really scientifically substantiate this in any factual way, but I feel it to be true. There are certainly those who doubt me. And that's okay. I know what I know—unless I don't know it...which is often the case.

I do know that there are many people who have talked about the varied levels of creatures (including humans) and the levels that they must move through as they progress through their spiritual lives. There are indeed lower creatures. For many years, here on earth in our own dimension, we have known that plants and trees have lives of sorts. They grow, they feed, they reproduce. Some people say they feel and communicate, and routinely talk to their plants and nurture them as beings. There are even those who worship them. Who is to say that there is, or is not, a style of communication or other form of interactive and intellectual ability attributed to these "beings?"

I believe that, in a lower dimension, an animal's life may begin as a "sort of" rock. I don't mean the kinds of rocks that we have in this dimension—though I suppose that even that is a possibility. I do know that this creature in the room at Mark's home is immobile—without feeling or any semblance of life in our way of describing existence. Yet it exists in another reality in a waiting form.

So, though changing in appearance and completely see-through as ghosts often are, this creature found sitting along the wall in the upstairs room at Mark's haunted house is nothing more than a rock from a lower dimension, waiting (possibly) to become an animal entity.

Checking into the room for the next few days via the Internet, I found the creature to be sitting in the same place, with the same face shifts. How long had this rock creature been waiting in the lower dimension? It did not know—nor did it even realize that I was communicating with it. How was it that we were seeing it from this dimension? It had not been there even two weeks prior. It did not know. I did not know. It only knew that it was sitting in the same spot. This meant to me that in this particular place, there was a chance that there was a bleed through of dimensions. Could a portal be beginning to appear at this very location? How would the rock creature be affected?

These questions were all unanswered with no real plausible way for explanation in the future—or at least until we understand more about dimensional shifts. Research continues on many fronts. Mark Sarro is in the forefront.

Or Was I Wrong?

So for the moment, with questions about the rock creature in my heart, I moved on to my normal routine. I began my Open Sessions again. But a surprise was in store for me.

My core group of animals had changed. Sadly, my helper, Cooneys, who was there to help me "do the good work" could not sit still for the nearly two months I'd been unable to communicate with them. I was unable to connect to her personally as I'd done so often before; rather I got the "knowing" that she was back with the D'Agostinos (her prior owners) doing the good work again. I couldn't tell whether she was in her ghostly state or had reincarnated back into a new animal that was now attached to them. This getting back the power was frustrating! Prior to the shut down, such knowledge was easy to get. Now, it was a struggle.

Solo, my horse friend, though in and out, was not the upstanding attendee either at this juncture. He had pastures to scour and other things to keep him busy. My own Tessa was off in yellow-flowered fields and not quite so prominent, for this was before the great Spiderman switch. My two dogs, Rufus and Spiderman, were never strong in the group, but were less so now, both deep into their lives at the Roseberry household. They were still in the group, but also less visible. None of this was a true surprise, since I'd been unavailable to them for so long.

Of course, Bentley remained a mainstay, full of orders and affections. Looking back, it was a surprise that this crotchety bird had become such a wonderful friend and confidant. We'd been through much, this feathered friend and me. Mary's three cats, speaking in one voice most of the time, were there, though they were quiet and spent most of their time just observing the group.

A Visitor to Open Session

The real surprise came with the new member. One January afternoon, I opened the session and found the rock creature sitting there at the edge of the semi-circle.

Bentley was crotchety again. "What the hell's this thing?" he said to me before I could say a word. He marched his little self over to it and kicked it with his little foot.

"It's a rock creature, Bentley," I told him. "I came across it when I was in the ITC Lounge."

"I know *that*," he remarked with bitter tone. "What's it doing here in my group?"

"*Our* group," I corrected. "And I really don't know. I'm as surprised as you are. It doesn't speak or know anything at all. I don't know how it got here." I watched Bentley kick it again.

"A rock," he said, and then looked back at me. "Get rid of it; we don't need no dam rock."

Mary's cats were giggling.

"Do you think it's spying on us," Bentley asked seriously. "That could happen ya know."

I didn't think so, though I didn't know how that kind of thing went. Did rocks from a lower dimension have the ability to spy?

"I don't think this is something we need to worry about Bentley, or I'd have that feeling. My guides are right there next to it and they wouldn't allow any of us to be hurt. Don't know why the rock is here, but since it is, it can stay."

Bentley glared at the guides as if he wasn't entirely sure they, too, were not spies of some sort. In defiance, and I believe to show that he was still in control of most things, he hopped up on top of the rock and perched there. "Why does its face change like that. Can't it decide what it wants to be? Doesn't it know that it can choose?"

Hmm. The bird was smart (of course, I already knew that). "I don't think it does know that it can choose. Or, if it does know, it may be trying to decide which animal it likes best," I told Bentley and the group.

Gracie spoke up, independent of the other two cats. "I think it should be a cat." Then she directed her voice to the rock. "You should be a cat."

Although Bentley can often be seen giving his favorite characters attention, he wasn't real sure about the Rock Creature. *Photo courtesy of Marla Brooks.*

Bentley said, "It should be a bird; why not a bird?"

"Cat," said the three cats as one voice.

"Bird," said Bentley.

I interrupted. "It doesn't seem to have the choice of bird, Bentley. It changes from cat to rat to raccoon. Sometimes I think I see a fox, too, though I'm not sure."

"Cat," said the cats.

Bentley kicked out at the rock again. "Stupid rock."

In sessions after the fact, the rock sat without contribution, but Bentley had now taken to sitting on it because the rock, for Bentley, maintains a warm surface on which he can warm his feet. Marla told me that this made sense to her because Bentley is well known for sitting on the slightly warm cable TV box to keep his feet warm. Knowing that this was something that Bentley would respond positively to, does this mean that rocks have an intellectual side that we cannot comprehend? Those I've talked to in the paranormal world think that this is a distinct possibility.

So why was the rock there in my Open Session group? I had the feeling that though it could not interact on my terms exactly and knew nothing of itself, it was there to absorb a kind of learning and that it felt akin to me because I'd tried to move it up a notch "on the proverbial food chain." (Or rock chain.) I'd recognized it and was there to help.

A member of the ITC Lounge chat room told me that she'd begun dreaming about the rock, though she hadn't a clue why, visualizing it as a raccoon hit by a car and not knowing what to do next. She'd thought about it a lot and thought that maybe she was seeing the rock's future or past, and that maybe that it was actually a spirit of an animal and not a rock at all.

This, too, was possible—since no one really knows—but the ITC devices kept picking up the word *rock* on the days we were there online discussing it. This indicates that the rock portion of the story is definitely important somehow.

But regardless of the reason that it was there and what it really was, I had a new member in the Core Group.

Upcoming sessions would be interesting. If nothing else, they would be rock solid.

Zira the Heroine

Unfortunately, there are other things in the ITC Lounge and around Mark Sarro's house that cause trouble for the animals in the house. Mark has a wonderful dog, Zira, who has been a joy since I first met Mark many years ago in the early ghost investigative years. What everyone remembers best about Zira is her poor digestive system—she can clear a room in seconds. Our ghost meetings and training sessions at Mark's

Zira has had many paranormal run-ins with the ghosts at Mark's house. She's had to pull him out of the haunted room when negative things began to happen there.

home were always filled with laughter due to Zira's digestive antics. I must say here, though, that this was a loving dog, too—she was a delight with her happy disposition, and had a wagging tail that could knock you down.

Oddly, though, having all these interactions over the prior years with Zira, I hadn't contacted

her to practice my animal communication skills. Even with all the hub-bub of the Lounge and the dark investigation, I'd not thought to do it. Bentley kept me quite busy.

One day, during my Open Session, however, Zira was there. I was so surprised and greeted her warmly.

But, of course, there was a somber reason she was visiting me this day. It was the man in the plaid shirt. She asked me to please tell Mark to tell this ghost not to bother her. The ghost did not like her, she said to me, and didn't really like dogs period. As she spoke to me, I saw in my mind a red plaid shirt worn by a dark-skinned man.

At the next meeting (which was that very weekend), I spoke to Mark about it. Such a ghost had indeed been seen and described the way

Zira said. It was alive and well in Mark's house, continually causing disturbances of one sort or another. I told Mark that this ghost always scared Zira by touching her when she least expected it, making her scurry to hide from the unseen hands. She also told me that she'd had to pull Mark from the room upstairs (the ITC Lounge), barking ferociously when the door was closed and something was going on in there that was to Mark's detriment. We'd seen such an incident on the video feed.

Everyone in the CCPRS ghost investigative group expects more to come to pass in the ITC Lounge—it just needs to be monitored and researched carefully. (The BBC American network television show, *Primeval* comes to mind. Rocks, monsters, and ghosts—Oh my!)

9. Animal Shorts

"Then God commanded,
Let the earth produce all kinds of animal life;
domestic and wild, large and small, and it was done.
So God made them all, and
He was pleased with what He saw."

~Genesis 1:24, 25

Never Too Late for a Mistake — George, Angus, and Elwood

Immediately after I took the Anita Curtis training, I went out seeking subjects to practice my new-found talent upon. You know already how well Bentley assisted me at that time, and even Mary's cats; but prior to them, I placed my confidence in three very special Boston Terriers who frequented my workplace.

For those who work at Schiffer Publishing, it was common knowledge who had the power there—it was George. George, a brown and white Boston Terrier, was everyone's supervisor and followed his master, Peter (my boss), around everyplace he went. If you saw Peter, you knew that George was right there. If you saw George, it was a certainty

George and Pete Schiffer working. You can surely tell whose in charge.

that Peter would be in your sight right after. They were an inseparable team.

George is a big boy—hearty and stout, with a lovely brown dot on the top of his head, and eyes that can see into your soul. And he is in charge. Each morning, as Peter made his rounds to find out how each employee was doing and what their needs were for the day, George also interacted with us.

It was very clear, however, that a visit by George was one of a king visiting his subjects. It was a necessary responsibility.

The Boston boys, Elwood and Angus, have been known to run through the offices at Schiffer Publishing as though chased by demons.

He was somewhat stand-offish until one knew that he wore the crown and was due the respect. Once that was established, this proud pup would let down his guard—just a tad—to accept a special dog snack or the occasional neck rub. But he let it be known that there would be no hanky-panky at the office as long as he were there keeping an eye on things. George was a pillar. And I loved him from the very first time I met him.

Angus and Elwood….now here was a different story. These two Boston boys belonged to Peter's son, Pete, and they often came to visit the office. Beautiful boys, too, they were George's sons, smaller in stature and black and white in color. These were the wild boys! You could often see them tearing through the building, running at what seemed ninety miles an hour, one right after the other, on a mission to….well, to do whatever it was they felt they needed to run that fast to do.

At first, around me, they seemed a bit skittish. I always spoke to the animals, even before this new talent had developed. But when I spoke to these guys, they would stop in their tracks, look at me in horror, howl, and then run like hell to get away from what they must have seen as the beast from beyond. I didn't get it. Animals always loved me. But these two seemed to be terrified of my presence in the beginning. Little by little, I'd see them here and there around the office and they began to make small gestures of contact as they got used to me. Still, I did not have the same relationship with them as I did with George. These two merely tolerated me and my baby talk. (Yes, I'm one of those who talk to animals like babies.)

At any rate, on the first day back at work after my training, I came out of my office and there stood Angus and Elwood. They eyed me carefully. Here was a chance, I thought to myself. Let me just go back in my office, do a quick elevator ritual, and talk to these two rambunctious guys. Surprisingly, it was easy to make contact with them. I saw them clearly in my mind, standing at attention, a bit perplexed, but waiting for what would happen next.

"Hi," I said to them. "I just took a class to learn to talk to animals and wanted to talk to you."

No response; they just stood there with tilted heads.

I continued. "I just wanted to let you know how beautiful you are and that I love you. I really like seeing you here at the office."

Then, in my vision, they began to bounce about and both came to me, jumping and licking and showing me affection. They never said a word; it was just a show of affection. I left the vision.

I walked out of my office then and toward our small kitchen where the two dogs were now standing. As soon as they saw me, they tore toward me and began reacting to me in the same fashion as the vision. They were rolling on their backs, offering their bellies for rubs and kissing me with great wet tongues. I was laughing at this new way they were acting; it was wonderful!

Then I looked up from them. George was standing off to one side. And oddly, Peter was not in sight. George looked angry. He stared right into my eyes for a couple seconds. I called to him, and instead of coming as he'd always done in the past, he turned and walked away, never once looking back. It was clear. He was furious with me.

"George, wait!" I called, "I love you, too! Don't go!"

He disappeared around the corner. Oh well, I thought. I should be more careful. I'll just communicate with him, too. Easily fixed.

Not.

When I tried to go down into my mode, I could see him there, but he had his back to me and would not speak, nor would he turn to look at me. My guides just shook their heads. So early in the game, and I'd not been careful about the relationships I'd already developed. George was angry because I'd shown favoritism to other dogs over him—he who was the almighty one.

I'd created a great sin in his dog eyes. Making amends would not be that easy.

I, of course, kept trying. George was "the man!" I couldn't have him mad at me. I continued to try to communicate. He continued to ignore me. When Peter came around to talk to me—multiple times a day—George would not even come into my office, but instead, sat outside or went to visit someone else to kill time until Peter left me. Nothing I could do worked. This went on for about two months. He just would not forgive me. I made sure that I didn't make over the other two dogs excessively and never when George was in ear or eye shot.

Finally, one morning, Peter passed my office to visit someone else, and George was following behind. He, as usual now, ignored me as he passed by. I went down into my communication mode. Begging for forgiveness, I professed my love for this great small creature. I apologized and told him that I was just trying to learn how to communicate with animals and was practicing on Angus and Elwood. I'd been so happy to learn that I could do it. It in no way had I meant that my feelings for him had changed.

When I lifted my head, he was standing outside my office looking in at me.

"George…" I whispered.

Then, in as clear a communications statement that could be made, he turned his back on me, standing there showing me his tail end. The message was oh so obvious.

"Come on, George," I coaxed. "Please forgive me."

He turned around and looked at me, thought about it a few seconds, and tentatively walked into my office. Allowing me about three seconds to scratch his neck, he turned and left. I'd been forgiven. Well, sorta kinda.

There was a price to pay. Though George had forgiven me to an extent, he still never regained his trust or affection for me in the same way as before. I'd damaged the relationship just as if I'd been a cheating spouse. Yes, he allowed me to rub him, even scratch his belly from time to time, but he never went out of his way again. I was merely part of the Schiffer furniture in his little eyes. I'd made a grave error in judgement. Consequences and payments ran high.

As I prepare this manuscript, I wonder will he ever feel the same again. Will he ever forgive me totally? Angus and Elwood no longer run from me or howl in my presence. They come to visit and show their obvious happiness at seeing me. But I'm careful now. I do not communicate with them on that special level. That won't happen until I can convince George that all are God's creatures and that there is plenty of love to go around.

And this might take some time…

George now mourns Peter…and though I'd worried about our relationship at the writing of this book, now all is forgiven. He's my buddy again.

174

The Cool Coolidge Pup — Rob Roy

During a formal ghost investigation with the Chester County Paranormal Research Society at the Hall of Presidents in Gettysburg, Pennsylvania, I saw a lovely copy of a painting of First Lady Grace Coolidge (for President Calvin Coolidge, 1923-1929), posing with a beautiful white dog on thc White House lawn. The lady figure and the painting was located on the second floor in the display area entitled the Hall of the First Ladies. The original painting is displayed in the China Room at the White House.

The figures of the ladies were not exact replicas of the women, but rather a way to display the beautiful inauguration gowns which indicated the styles of varied eras. The paintings or photos above the "dolls," however, were the true essences of the women depicted. This, then, was where my attention was drawn—to Grace Coolidge and the white dog that stared lovingly up at her, shown in the photograph of the painting above her statue.

When we first took basic readings during the mapping phase of our investigation, we found that there

Rob Roy, Calvin Collidge's sheep hearding dog, spoke to me at the Hall of President's exhibit of the First Ladies in Gettysburg, Pennsylvania. This image shows the likeness of First Lady Grace and a photo of her and Rob Roy placed directly above her.

were no EMF (electromagnetic field) disturbances in the rooms housing the figures, which might indicate ghostly goings-on. However, many times throughout the evening, and also on this second floor, we found that EMF readings would come and go sporadically, indicating a possible fluctuation in the air that would indicate paranormal activity. We did believe that, in most cases, this was due to electrical outlets, etc.

But during one instance, the flashing EMF meter in my hand was a true indicator of something going on in the world beyond. By the figure of the First Lady Grace Coolidge and the painting above her illustrating her and the beautiful white dog, the EMF readings spiked and then remained constant. I felt the presence of this magnificent dog.

Making an effort to use animal communications to get in touch with the animal, but having little information, I was uncertain as to the questions to ask. I was only able to see the dog running and jumping in the grass (as any dog possibly) on the front lawn of the White House at a time of the year where the grass was bright and green. It was a prominent thought—the importance of being outside running and jumping and playing, as though dogs were made for romping and not for socializing inside. The EMF meter continued to flash in front of the case where the painting was located.

The interesting, and telling, part of this was that the EMF readings showing were not indicative of the Base readings we'd taken earlier showing that the room was "at rest." It seemed that these new readings around the painting were true changes to the atmosphere and possibly paranormal in nature. I feel that it was directly linked to the dog. I was pulled time and again to this spot as though there were more things that the dog wanted to relate, but my mind was on ghosts in general and not specifically on just the dog.

Once the investigation was over, and days later, I could not get the image of this dog out of my mind. I wondered whether there were records of

Close up of the photo of First Lady Grace and Rob Roy.

him, so I searched online. I found that the Coolidge household was a prime home for animals, with both the president and first lady loving both cats and dogs. These animals graced the White House property throughout the Coolidge administration. In fact, the painting I'd seen (once hung in the Red Room prior to its current location in the China Room) was given to the United States by the Pi Beta Phi Fraternity.

The dog who'd taken my heart that night at the Hall of Presidents was Rob Roy, a sheep-herding dog from Wisconsin. Of course, there weren't many sheep grazing on the White House lawn, so Rob Roy was a bit out of his element. In fact, it has been noted in the varied articles mentioning Rob that his time inside was often in turmoil—he loved to be outside. This was where he enjoyed life the most.

As animals do, Rob Roy finally did become accustomed to being indoors as well as out, but it was obvious that it was his joy to take walks outside on the property, and it was expected that he was ready to race and play at a moment's notice when the opportunity arose. Chasing squirrels was a special treat. He was even known to be a boating dog, accompanying the president on fishing excursions.

Rob Roy died of a stomach ailment in 1928, and was revered as a "stately companion of great courage and fidelity" by Calvin Coolidge. This was a great family loss for Grace and Calvin.

Would I be able to contact Rob Roy? I certainly was in touch that night at the Hall of Presidents, but with a full investigation going on, I hadn't had the mental fortitude to really connect. What about now? Would this majestic dog find me interesting enough to talk with?

As I relaxed in my office chair, looking at the photo I'd taken of Grace and Rob Roy, I got the immediate vision of the dog crouching down with his front legs as though ready to pounce. He was in a field of green grass and tall yellow and white flowers.

"I saw you that night," he said to me. "Thank you for calling me beautiful. That man with you was not so nice. I do not have mange."

One of the other investigators had not been impressed with the painting and made mention that the dog appeared to have mange. I reprimanded him for such a statement. This was a beautiful dog.

"I loved my time with them [Coolidges] and I am with them again—though now I stay in the fields—I love the fields. I am well, but I will not be back. I will stay here. I am happy here."

Then Rob Roy said something that startled me.

"I played with your dog in the fields today. I knew you were coming to talk to me." At that moment, I saw in my mind's eye, both Rob Roy and my little dog, Tessa, romping in the flowers, having a good ol' time.

Rob Roy ended with, "I was the best White House dog."

And I was inclined to agree.

Animals in the Wild

A Snake in the Grass—Gulp!

At one point in my investigation of the strange and creepy in the area, I came across Jesse Rothacker, the founder of Forgotten Friend Reptile Sanctuary in Lancaster County, Pennsylvania. I personally couldn't think of a more creepy animal to communicate with than a snake. (Now I don't want email on this, folks—everyone is creeped out by *some*thing!)

There was even a part of me that questioned my desire to consider it. But alas, I knew that I'd watched way too many giant snake movies on the Sci Fi channel and that was coloring my viewpoint. Still....

Jessie has had snake experiences that are very odd—and frankly scary to me. He's found them in the sidings of homes and seen them slither through to interior cupboards and such. They've been found inside dishwashers, in cars (the one in the car actually made its way up to the front seat while a friend of his was on the turnpike—now there's an accident waiting to happen!), abandoned in apartments, and there was even a lady who used snakes to assault police

Snakes, at least this one, are not terribly talkative. Lucky to be rescued, this guy is (as of this writing) part of the Forgotten Friend Reptile Sanctuary in Lancaster County, Pennsylvania.
Photo courtesy of Jessi Rothacker.

officers (beyond the call of duty for the "boys in blue," I'd say).

He advised me that the area I was researching (in Lancaster County at the time) had both native (wild) and exotic (pet) species. There were lots of calls about giant pythons and alligators as well. Did I really want to do this?

At any rate, he sent me a photo of a nice big boa, who was rescued by the Lancaster Humane League, so that I might communicate with it. I swallowed hard when I first saw the photo. Oh my. This was a scary job, but someone had to do it. Or some such *patriotic* saying that I could use to convince myself that I could open my mind up to a … gulp… snake.

So I went into my meditative state. My guides were laughing at me. The Lemur was actually rolling on the ground. Both thought my fear silly. This was one of God's creatures. Why was I afraid? Hadn't they seen the movie, *Anaconda*?

I started, as usual, by focusing in on the snake, and introducing myself. I let it know that I knew its history of being rescued. The communication was instant.

From the snake: "What. [a flat statement but not nearly a question.] No food. Better now. Eat.

I asked: "Do you have or did you have a relationship with your caretakers?"

From the snake: "Relationship. No."

I said, "People tend to think that snakes do have relationships. Some have your kind as pets…"

From the snake: "No. Food. Provide easy food while captive. Food. Easy food. Go away. No more talk."

And that was it. It was creepy. Not a creature for long inspirational chat. I was inclined (despite Jesse's instruction otherwise) to believe the *Anaconda* movie.

To learn more about Jesse and his critters, visit: Forgotten Friend Reptile Sanctuary at www.forgottenfriend.org.

What Are Ya? Nuts?

This next story of animals in the wild is short but telling. One thing that Gerri Gassert, from my early training class, and I have in common is that we hate to see animals killed on the roads. It affects both of us greatly. And we both send out blessings to those we see dead on the highways of the world, victims of fast-moving traffic.

Most times, these blessings are offered after the fact by hours, or days. The animal has been smushed and then has lain there until the birds or nature's other methods turn the small body back to the earth. I've even been known to offer a warm thought to the leftover fur of a months-old road kill.

But one day, Gerri witnessed a squirrel's demise at the hands of a driver right in front of her—an on-the-spot occurrence. Her heart went up into her mouth as her remorse and sadness filled the air. She blessed the tiny creature.

And, for the first time for Gerri, the squirrel heard the blessing the moment it was uttered. Yes, it was quite dead and now just a passing vision in her rear view mirror, but it's spirit stuck for a moment.

"What?!" it said to her with sarcastic muse. "You think that was an accident? You think that I didn't want that to happen? You think that life is so easy here that I want to stay here? I ran out in front of that machine on purpose! I wanted to move on! How stupid do you think we are? We know what's on the other side! Stupid humans."

And he was gone.

Now that put a whole new spin on things. For me, it was an alien way to think. Suicidal squirrels… this required more thought.

Conclusion: What's It All About...Bentley?

"Outta the mouths of birds...I mean babes..."

~(Doesn't everyone say this?)

I think it would be apropos to close this exploration of the mysteries of ghosts and pets with yet another strange session that began with a visit to the ITC Lounge at the very haunted West Chester, Pennsylvania, house where the spirit of the rock creature sits waiting.

Investigator and cat woman, Mary Gasparo and psychic Laurie Hull spent some late evening time in front of their computers, alone peering into the haunted room, finding this to be very productive. I say productive in an uneasy sense, because it wasn't a very good productive time—rather a (gulp) scary kinda thing.

While watching their computer screens, with cameras switching back and forth showing the room with all its gloominess and pixilation, they began seeing shadows and darting forms. In their own homes, in their own office chairs, as they watched the screen, their own locations were coming alive as well. It was as though the spirits of the room came through the lines and settled into their previously warm environments.

A chill centered at both Laurie and Mary's homes that eventually forced them to shut down their computers.

That night and into the next day, they became the victims of a physical haunting so strange that it had them creeping around their homes looking for prowlers and staying glued to each other on the phone, each promising to call 911 for the other, should the worse happen.

But it wasn't prowlers in their homes. It was possible that they'd brought a ghost (or ghosts) from the haunted room into their own lives. Hearing banging and knocking from inside closets and from behind locked doors, listening to the movement of heavy furniture in rooms where nothing was out of place, and generally a chilled feeling that they were not alone prevailed throughout the day. Laurie had gotten psychically a specific name: Victor.

Mary emailed me at work, to let me know the latest development—they were being haunted! (Do you now understand my prior warnings regarding this

Bentley knows his stuff. Bentley knows what life is about. Bentley is in charge. *Photo courtesy of Marla Brooks.*

kind of thing?) There was nothing I could do, of course; and eventually, their homes calmed down.

This is just a preamble to what I have to say next. On my way home from work, I began my typical Open Session. As the elevator door opened, my guides were there, as were Mary's three cats perched on chairs, Bentley standing on the rock, my own little Tessa, and Rufus.

I said, "Okay, here we go. Who needs to talk to me?"

Mary's cat, Belle, jumped up. "Me! Me! Me! Pick me!"

Bentley grumbled and the others stayed still as Belle began. In a sing-song voice, Belle said, "My Mommy is doing something she's not supposed to be doing."

Bentley mumbled, "Big mouth." He eyed Belle and saw her sway in excitement.

"Don't touch my rock," he yelled.

I had mixed emotions regarding asking about this. One issue that animal communicators must be very cognizant of is that animals will sometimes tell things that they are not supposed to tell. (Guides don't shut them down unless it's the big stuff.) Animals will blab secrets pretty routinely. So do I ask or should I not? What is ethical? In lieu of Mary's email to me that afternoon, I decided I'd risk asking. I didn't think we had many secrets between us anyway, so what the heck?

"Well," I said, "is what she doing harmful to her?"

"It could be," answered Belle, "because she keeps thinking about it. You're not supposed to think about it."

This brought to mind immediately a prior session with Bentley when he'd admonished Pipsqueak for telling about the portal. He'd also said that they were not supposed to talk about it because if they did, it would see them.

"Are you talking about what's going on in her house now? The ghost banging and keeping her on edge?" I asked gently, not wanting to scare the cat.

"Yup. She keeps thinkin' and thinkin' and thinkin' about it." The other cats were just nodding as Belle spoke.

"Do you know who it is?" I asked.

Bentley piped up now. "I think it might be one of my Mom's…but I'm not sure. We don't think about it."

"Do you know why it's here, Bentley? Just what is it?" I wanted to know.

Bentley looked pensive—as pensive as a bird could look, anyway. "You really don't know, do you? All this time and you don't know…"

I waited. He was quite dramatic and needed a full effect. He flexed his feet on the rock.

"When someone dies, at first they are confused. And sometimes that's who these ghosts are. But the confusion doesn't last long and then the soul knows everything. It doesn't need to come back here to talk to us. So those that do need to talk to us from the other side, haven't gotten through the confused state or they haven't moved on to the next level yet. Some wait in the quiet, like my rock, some are loud and scary like the ones we don't think about."

Wow. The bird knew his stuff.

"But others come back from time to time to visit…" I suggested, hoping this was true because otherwise I was totally off on the good ghost theories.

"Well yeah," he answered sarcastically. "But you wanted to know why *this one* was here."

I nodded. It made sense in the scheme of things—for me anyway. I'd always wondered why some people who you thought might come back as ghosts, people who promised they would, don't. It's because they don't need to. They understand everything at that point and know that it doesn't help us in any constructive way to interact any longer.

Those we sense at hauntings are either still in their initial confused state, or at a level of existence where they, too, are still struggling to learn about …well, whatever it is that we need to know on the other side. *We* are the other side to them.

So I conclude this collection of events with a question: What do you believe about life on the other side, animal communications, or psychic ability? What do you need to know? How do the animals fit into the scheme of things?

Bentley knows the secrets of life—and death. Wow. That's *gotta* scare ya.

Appendix 1: The Do's and Don'ts in Animal Communication

"Speak up for those who cannot speak for themselves. Protect the rights of all who are helpless."

~ Proverbs 31:8

🦴 Do Research and understand the phases of grief. For those of you wishing to try animal communications, please realize that in addition to the communications, you will also be learning human counseling involving grief, how to listen to those in pain, and methods of communicating that are beneficial to those you talk with as a whole. If you don't, you can cause more grief than help. (Remember the Wiccan way: *Harm ye none*.)

🦴 Don't ever think that your advice can replace that of a veterinarian. This is not a science. You can at best assist or suggest direction for the owner to discuss with the animal's vet.

🦴 Do practice, practice, practice. It's the only way you train your brain—which may fight you every step of the way in some cases.

🦴 Don't get too high on your abilities—they aren't yours anyway, only lent to you by your higher being.

🦴 Do learn to use the pendulum. It is an invaluable tool.

⊂⊃ Don't believe everything the pendulum tells you. It's only a backup measure and there are too many variables to make it totally comprehensive all the time.

⊂⊃ Do interact with others in the paranormal world including psychics, mediums, and ghost people for varied slants. They also provide great encouragement for the most part.

⊂⊃ Don't compare yourself to the above-mentioned paranormal people as they will most likely see your world as muted or unscientific—there could be contention. None of it is important to you. You are what you are.

⊂⊃ Do pray. If you don't ask, how will you know what you will get?

⊂⊃ Don't go into any situation without prayers and protections first. You never know what could happen.

⊂⊃ Do practice varied methods of meditation until the right one for you surfaces. The first method, or my way, may not be the right one for you.

⊂⊃ Don't be discouraged if those around you are not as supportive as you might like. This is always the way in spiritual matters—people will doubt you as you may doubt yourself. Listening to them only makes the job more difficult.

⊂⊃ Do interact with other animal communicators and other spiritual people. You will find that being around like individuals will help your own skill.

⊂⊃ Don't think you have all the answers. As soon as you do, the questions will change and you will look like a fool. Or worse, make a mistake.

⊂⊃ Do try to teach others the skill. No need to be secretive or hold it close as though only you can contact the animals. This skill is for everyone and serves animals everywhere.

🦴 Don't ever turn someone in pain away. What goes around, comes around.

🦴 Do speak up and out about animal abuse. Join groups. Donate time and money. Become part of the solution.

🦴 Don't feel that you can save the world. We'd all like to do that, but it's just not possible. Just save the few you can.

🦴 Do read everything you can about spiritual well being and improvement, including developing your psychic powers and understanding the world beyond.

🦴 Don't believe everything you hear and read. Allow your own spirit to guide you.

🦴 Do, as per Tessa, practice forgiveness to live peacefully together with all God's creatures.

Murphy O'Reilley is a chunky Roseberry family member. He told animal communicator Gerri Gassert that he preferred to only eat wet food with the salmon flavor and that he hated Rufus yelling in his ears at dinner time. (Rufus is a barker and always barks for his food—yes, he's spoiled.)

Appendix 2: RAM: Random Animal Messages

"My journey is far from being over..."

~Lisa Williams, www.lisawilliams.com

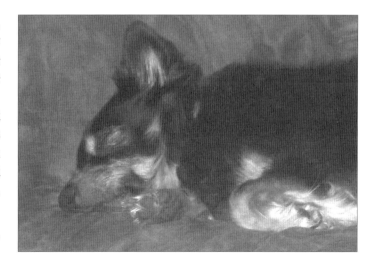

So, at the end of my research for this topic, I was given a strong suggestion from my guides. I was to *give back*. I was also given the method, though I'd not recognized it until the end and until it was pointed out to me.

Throughout my learning process and even past into my daily animal communications, I'd always found that strange animals would come to me from time to time. By strange, I mean, those I'd not tried to contact, and I didn't know or recognize.

Rufus participates in one of his favorite pastimes. Animal Communicators can talk to the animals even if they are sleeping. The animal soul (as ours) is always available for a conversation.

I'd always ask around to see if my current friends and clients knew of such an animal and though they struggled to come up with who the creature might be, it was futile and a final answer was never specific enough. No one recognized these animals in need beyond a guess.

Now, if you've learned nothing from my prose, let me just say that what follows is of great importance:

Things happen for a reason.
There are no coincidences.

Jackie, a work associate in my office, directed me to the Lisa Williams website. Lisa is a medium that I particularly like and respect. She, too, must have strangers touch her heart because she's formed a portion of her site to include random messages given to her about people who were not sitting in front of her requesting to be "read."

I knew immediately that I was to mirror this wonderful lady and give out to the world these varied animal messages. My guides were happy that I quickly recognized this epitome of thought. Too, I found that three animals from my core group would be giving messages and thoughts as well. You guessed it, Bentley would lead the pack guided by my two animal guides (much to his distaste). Solo the horse would be closely following to offer accurate precision, and Gracie the cat would offer spiritual guidance beyond the messages, if such was needed.

So there you have it. Starting at the end of August, 2009, my personal blog (attached to my website) will display a section entitled Random Animal Messages as long as I'm guided to provide it. I've no idea how many messages will come, when, or to what degree; but I will relay what the animals and spirit says to the best of my ability to whoever they apply to. I will record what I get, but cannot elaborate on any particular message beyond what I'm given. That's not the premise, here. The messages are what they are.

The best way to keep track of these messages is to visit routinely to see if any of them point to your particular situation.

Visit http://roseberrybooks.com and click on Random Animal Messages if you're on my website to find out about my other activities and projects, or http://blog.roseberrybooks.com for the actual blogging. Feel free to comment back!

Good luck and have fun with it. Hope it helps!

Note to Other Animal Communicators

Please feel free to send me your random messages for posting on my web blog as well. I will include your contact information as you desire. We're all here to help the animals, so I welcome the partnership.

http://roseberrybooks.com

http://blog.roseberrybooks.com

Bibliography and Website Resources

You've heard that in stressful situations people use the fight or flight response. This also applies to pastry. Bentley in flight to fight for his cake. *Photo courtesy of Marla Brooks.*

Curtis. Anita. *Animal Wisdom*. Lincoln, NE: IUniverse. com. 2006.

Detzler, Robert E. *The Freedom Path*. SRC Publishing: Lacy, WA, 2006.

A Tail to Tell: www.atailtotell.com.

Amish: en.wikipedia.org/wiki/Amish.

Anita Curtis: www.anitacurtis.com.

Chester County Paranormal Research Soci ety: www.chestercountyprs.com.

Chester County SPCA: www.ccspca.org.

Critter Chatter, Hope Pollock, Hopescritters@aol.com.

David Pietruza: www.davidpietrusza.com/coolidge-pets.html.

David Wells: www.davidwells.co.uk/#.

Dinah Roseberry: http://roseberrybooks.com.

Donna Doyle: www.donnadoolittle.com.

Ghost Quest: www.ghost-quest.org/.

Grace Coolidge: en.wikipedia.org/wiki/Grace_Coolidge.

Humane League of Lancaster County: www.humaneleague.com.

ITC: www.angelsghosts.com/instrumental_transcommunication.

ITC Lounge: www.livestream.com/itclounge.

Forgotten Friend Reptile Sanctuary. www.forgottenfriend.org.

Kaye Ames School for Dogs: www.kayeames.com.

Laurie Hull: www.delcoghosts.com.

Lee Prosser: www.ghostvillage.com/library/leeprosser.html.

Lisa J. Smith: www.forthesoulfromthesoul.com/lisajsmithhome.html.

Lisa Williams: www.lisawilliamsmedium.com/.

Longs Park, Lancaster, PA: www.longspark.org.

Marla Brooks: hauntedwriter.com/.

Mary Gasparo: www.myspace.com/catlady0702.

Para-X Radio. www.para-x.com.

PetFinders. www.petfinders.com.

Schiffer Publishing: www.schifferbooks.com and www.schifferghosts.com.

Thomas and Arlene D'Agostino: www.myspace.com/tomarlene.

Victoria Gross: www.tarotla.com/.

Wikipedia. http://en.wikipedia.org/wiki/Ostrich.